EYE ON
Art

GRAFFITI

by Michael V. Uschan

LUCENT BOOKS
A part of Gale, Cengage Learning

GALE
CENGAGE Learning

Detroit • New York • San Francisco • New Haven, Conn • Waterville, Maine • London

LIBRARY OF CONGRESS CATALOGING-IN-PUBLICATION DATA

Uschan, Michael V., 1948-
  Graffiti / by Michael V. Uschan.
    p. cm. -- (Eye on art)
  Includes bibliographical references and index.
  ISBN 978-1-4205-0324-1 (hardcover)
  1. Graffiti--Juvenile literature. I. Title.
  GT3912.U83 2010
  751.7'3--dc22

                                                    2010028699

Lucent Books
27500 Drake Rd
Farmington Hills MI 48331

ISBN-13: 978-1-4205-0324-1
ISBN-10: 1-4205-0324-3

Printed in the United States of America
1 2 3 4 5 6 7 14 13 12 11 10

Printed by Bang Printing, Brainerd, MN, 1st Ptg., 10/2010

CONTENTS

Foreword. 5

Introduction 8
What Is Graffiti?

Chapter 1 13
History of Graffiti

Chapter 2 28
The Birth of Modern Graffiti

Chapter 3 42
Graffiti's Golden Age

Chapter 4 56
Social and Political Graffiti

Chapter 5 71
How Modern Graffiti Spread

Chapter 6 85
Graffiti—Art or Vandalism?

Notes 100

For More Information 106

Index. 108

Picture Credits 112

About the Author. 112

Foreword

Some thirty-one thousand years ago, early humans painted strikingly sophisticated images of horses, bison, rhinoceroses, bears, and other animals on the walls of a cave in southern France. The meaning of these elaborate pictures is unknown, although some experts speculate that they held ceremonial significance. Regardless of their intended purpose, the Chauvet-Pont-d'Arc cave paintings represent some of the first known expressions of the artistic impulse.

From the Paleolithic era to the present day, human beings have continued to create works of visual art. Artists have developed painting, drawing, sculpture, engraving, and many other techniques to produce visual representations of landscapes, the human form, religious and historical events, and countless other subjects. The artistic impulse also finds expression in glass, jewelry, and new forms inspired by new technology. Indeed, judging by humanity's prolific artistic output throughout history, one must conclude that the compulsion to produce art is an inherent aspect of being human, and the results are among humanity's greatest cultural achievements: masterpieces such as the architectural marvels of ancient Greece, Michelangelo's perfectly rendered statue *David*, Vincent van Gogh's visionary painting *Starry Night*, and endless other treasures.

The creative impulse serves many purposes for society. At its most basic level, art is a form of entertainment or the means for a satisfying or pleasant aesthetic experience. But art's true power lies not in its potential to entertain and delight but in its ability to enlighten, to reveal the truth, and by doing so to uplift the human spirit and transform the human race.

One of the primary functions of art has been to serve religion. For most of Western history, for example, artists were paid by the church to produce works with religious themes and subjects. Art was thus a tool to help human beings transcend mundane, secular reality and achieve spiritual enlightenment. One of the best-known, and largest-scale, examples of Christian religious art is the Sistine Chapel in the Vatican in Rome. In 1508 Pope Julius II commissioned Italian Renaissance artist Michelangelo to paint the chapel's vaulted ceiling, an area of 640 square yards (535 sq. m). Michelangelo spent four years on scaffolding, his neck craned, creating a panoramic fresco of some three hundred human figures. His paintings depict Old Testament prophets and heroes, sibyls of Greek mythology, and nine scenes from the Book of Genesis, including the Creation of Adam, the Fall of Adam and Eve from the Garden of Eden, and the Flood. The ceiling of the Sistine Chapel is considered one of the greatest works of Western art and has inspired the awe of countless Christian pilgrims and other religious seekers. As eighteenth-century German poet and author Johann Wolfgang von Goethe wrote, "Until you have seen this Sistine Chapel, you can have no adequate conception of what man is capable of."

In addition to inspiring religious fervor, art can serve as a force for social change. Artists are among the visionaries of any culture. As such, they often perceive injustice and wrongdoing and confront others by reflecting what they see in their work. One classic example of art as social commentary was created in May 1937, during the brutal Spanish civil war. On May 1 Spanish artist Pablo Picasso learned of the recent attack on the small Basque village of Guernica by German airplanes allied with fascist forces led by Francisco Franco. The German pilots had used the village for target practice, a three-hour bombing that killed sixteen hundred civilians. Picasso, living in Paris, channeled his outrage over the massacre into his painting *Guernica,* a black, white, and gray mural that depicts dismembered animals and fractured human figures whose faces are contorted in agonized expressions. Initially, critics and the public condemned the painting as an incoherent hodgepodge, but the work soon came to be seen as a powerful antiwar statement and remains an iconic symbol of the violence and terror that dominated world events during the remainder of the twentieth century.

The impulse to create art—whether painting animals with crude pigments on a cave wall, sculpting a human form from marble, or commemorating human tragedy in a mural—thus serves many purposes. It offers an entertaining diversion, nourishes the imagination and the spirit, decorates and beautifies the world, and chronicles the age. But underlying all these functions is the desire to reveal that which is obscure—to illuminate, clarify, and perhaps ennoble. As Picasso himself stated, "The purpose of art is washing the dust of daily life off our souls."

The Eye on Art series is intended to assist readers in understanding the various roles of art in society. Each volume offers an in-depth exploration of a major artistic movement, medium, figure, or profession. All books in the series are beautifully illustrated with full-color photographs and diagrams. Riveting narrative, clear technical explanation, informative sidebars, fully documented quotes, a bibliography, and a thorough index all provide excellent starting points for research and discussion. With these features, the Eye on Art series is a useful introduction to the world of art—a world that can offer both insight and inspiration.

Introduction

What Is Graffiti?

In Los Angeles, California, a young man boldly prints the name of his street gang on the wall of a building to proclaim to the world that he and his friends rule the area. On the other side of the continent in New York City, a teenage girl uses a can of spray paint to create an elaborate signature whose crazily shaped letters and vibrant colors explode off a dingy, dull-colored wall to either amuse or annoy passersby. Thousands of miles south of both cities, two people in São Paulo, Brazil, are scrawling their names on a building which is already covered with hundreds of other similar markings. All three are examples of graffiti, which the Merriam-Webster OnLine Dictionary defines as "unauthorized writing or drawing on a public surface."[1]

Graffiti is a complex subject, one that many people have trouble understanding. Even the word itself is confusing. *Graffiti* is the plural form of *graffito*, a word that refers to one example of anything that meets the above definition. But the word *graffiti* is also a mass noun (a noun that refers to things that cannot be counted, like freedom or honesty), and it can be used in the singular. Further complicating the term are the various types of graffiti. Several varieties of graffiti are obscenities or gang names scrawled on walls or other flat surfaces, which most people consider vandalism. Graffiti, however, can be more than an illegal act of public vandalism. It is also a distinctive art form, one which graffiti artists cherish and believe other people should respect even if they do not understand or like it.

Scape Martinez is a San Jose, California, artist who became famous by adorning hundreds, perhaps thousands, of walls with his distinctive tag. *Tag* is the term graffiti artists use for the elaborate signatures they place on walls and other public areas. Martinez has created murals and other works that have been shown in prestigious art galleries, but he still reveres graffiti. Martinez believes graffiti is "a uniquely American art form" and claims its power stems from the fact that it is displayed publicly so that many people can see and be touched by it. He says, "[Graffiti] is a visual narrative [that] directly connects the street corner to the spirit, bypassing the definitions of art presented by art galleries and museums."[2]

A young man paints graffiti on a wall. The dictionary defines graffiti as "unauthorized drawing on a public surface," but the term is far more complex than this definition.

However, Martinez is only partially correct when he says that graffiti is an American art form. Although colorful graffiti did originate in the United States, other forms of graffiti existed for thousands of years before the country was created.

Self-Expression

Art historians say the first graffiti was done thirty thousand years ago when primitive people drew pictures and designs on cave walls. Thousands of years later when people began to communicate through a written language, writing appeared on public spaces. This written graffiti included everything from philosophical and political statements to crude and even obscene jokes. Examples of such graffiti from Egypt and the Roman Empire survived for several thousand years because they were often etched into stone or wood.

Until the late twentieth century, graffiti consisted mainly of words, often no more than someone's name. People sometimes added small drawings, some of them as beautiful as any

Ancient drawings on cave walls, such as this one in Moab, Utah, are considered to be the first examples of graffiti.

traditional art created at the time. But in the late 1960s and early 1970s, a new style of graffiti appeared in New York City that was much more creative, vibrant, and noticeable. Young people, mostly from poor black and Hispanic neighborhoods, began creating elaborate, multicolored copies of their tags. Most tags were done in spray paint and appeared on the sides of buildings, bridges, and other flat surfaces. Graffiti artists even began tagging subway cars and buses, which became giant mobile works of art that were viewed by millions of people as they traveled through the giant city.

The artists who initiated the modern graffiti that is still popular today referred to themselves as "writers" even though their work was far more artistic than mere printed letters. Unlike previous graffiti, the words splashed on various surfaces with markers and spray paint were not written in simple letters. Instead these tags, along with the symbols and caricatures that sometimes accompanied them, were artistically and whimsically designed. In *The Faith of Graffiti*, the landmark 1974 book that helped introduce the new art form to the world, famed novelist Norman Mailer comments on the creative ways in which writers twisted and distorted letters to make their tags true works of art. He writes, "What a quintessential marriage of cool and style to write your name in giant separate living letters, large as animals, lithe as snakes, mysterious as Arabic and Chinese curls of alphabet."[3]

The motivation graffiti artists had for doing graffiti was the same one that led cavepeople to cover walls with primitive paintings—a desire to communicate with other people and leave a record of their existence. Author Stephen Powers explains this need in his book *The Art of Getting Over: Graffiti at the Millennium*. He writes,

> If you've ever walked down the street, seen a name, and wondered what the marking meant, I'll tell you: It means somebody is telling you a story about who they are and what they are prepared to do to make you aware of it. Every time a name is written, a story gets told. It's a short story: "I was here."[4]

Despite the efforts of graffiti artists to make themselves known, the names they plaster on walls, buildings, and subway cars are not their real names. They use street aliases because they know they are doing something illegal.

Criminal Act or Art?

When modern graffiti began emerging in the 1960s and 1970s, public officials, businesspeople, and civic leaders routinely condemned it because the artists never asked permission to use the public spaces that became canvases for their work. Graffiti artists were considered trespassers on public and private property, and their work was labeled vandalism instead of art. An editorial in a Philadelphia, Pennsylvania, newspaper on May 20, 1974, condemned graffiti, saying: "Despite what some advanced thinkers suggest is a new art form, graffiti in its mindless scrawls on city walls is ugly, ugly, ugly. These idiotic and sleazy scrawls are criminal and have to be treated as such."[5]

The article summed up the negative attitudes many people had toward graffiti—it was vandalism that was an eyesore and a nuisance, and it was expensive to remove from surfaces that had been illegally decorated. This attitude toward graffiti still prevails today for the same reasons, even though some artists now work only on spaces for which they have permission.

Despite the negatives, modern graffiti developed into a powerful form of creative expression that grew in popularity in the United States and has since spread around the world. Henry Chalfant is a coauthor of *Subway Art*, a 1984 book about how the graffiti movement exploded after artists began tagging subway cars in New York in the 1970s. In the twenty-fifth anniversary edition of the book published in 2009, he describes how graffiti has flourished since 1984 and become a global phenomenon instead of one confined to New York. Chalfant writes, "[The] graffiti movement is alive and well in the world. There is a community of artists and enthusiasts who cross all borders and, with the Internet and affordable travel available to young people, graffiti has become an international youth culture."[6]

History of Graffiti

The bold, colorful images people have been painting on buildings and other public spaces since the 1970s are only the latest incarnation of the age-old practice of graffiti. In the book *Encyclopedia of Graffiti*, authors Robert Reisner and Lorraine Wechsler point out that this ancient art has been practiced for tens of thousands of years. "Graffiti," they write, "have been with us since prehistoric man placed his hand on a cave wall and traced the outlines of his fingers with pigment. It was his way of saying 'I exist.'"[7] That driving need to make one's identity known to the world has motivated people ever since those prehistoric times, including modern graffiti artists who create their bright, neon works mainly to make famous the street they have adopted.

In another book on graffiti, *Graffiti: Two Thousand Years of Wall Writing*, Reisner expands on why he believes people from prehistoric times to today have felt compelled to leave a record, written or drawn, for others to view. Reisner writes,

> Man is a natural communicator. A thought occurs to someone suddenly, or something is experienced during the day, and there is a compulsion to express it, if not

to another person, then to whatever is close at hand: paper, wall, rock, tree, door. Graffiti, then, are little insights, little peepholes into the minds of individuals who are spokesmen not only for themselves but for others like them.[8]

Reisner's belief that modern graffiti can be linked to prehistoric art is shared by most art historians. According to this theory, the earliest graffiti was made thirty thousand or more years ago. The images those primitive people drew or etched into stone were the only way they could leave a lasting record of what they sought to communicate to other people, because written language had not yet been invented.

Prehistoric Graffiti

Prehistoric art is commonly referred to as rock art because the art was often created on, or made from, rock that has survived to modern times. Although millions of rock-art sites are scattered across the globe, they are mainly found in Africa, Australia, and Europe. The art that has survived for millennia depicts images ranging from geometric designs and unidentified abstract symbols to scenes of people and animals. These images were either scratched into rock with crude tools, such as animal bones, or painted with simple pigments—primitive paints made by mixing a powdered substance with liquid to produce color—or even blood.

In December 1994 one of the most famous collections of prehistoric art was discovered in southeast France. The Chauvet-Pont-d'Arc cave is notable because some of the hundreds of drawings that cover its walls include animals that today are found only in Africa and had never been portrayed in previously found European rock art. French prehistoric art expert Jean Clottes viewed the cave shortly after it was discovered, and the drawings amazed him. He says, "The recognizable creatures painted in red included several rhinos, bears, and lions [and] one was indisputably a leopard, recognizable by its spots and its tail, which was devoid of the tuft all lions possess.

The leopard is the first known example of its kind [in cave art]."[9]

The Chauvet cave drawings are believed to have been done twenty thousand years ago, but some prehistoric art is thought to be much older. Despite the difficulty in accurately dating such work, rock art in Australia is estimated to be forty to fifty thousand years old. Among the Chauvet drawings are outlines of hands the artists made by blowing pigment on them through hollowed-out bones. Reisner writes, "I take these hand prints as evidence of man's drive to leave his impress [mark] upon the universe."[10]

The art in the Chauvet cave is well preserved because it is inside, which protects it from the elements. However, most prehistoric art sites have been found in open-air spaces—just

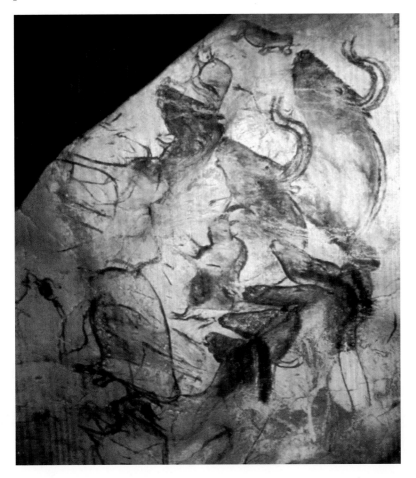

Prehistoric paintings on the wall of a cave in France depict horses and buffalo.

as graffiti is usually found in public spaces so other people can see it—where wind, water, and erosion have combined over the centuries to destroy much of the original art.

For thousands of years, such simple drawings were the only way people could leave a lasting imprint of their thoughts and feelings. Gradually, however, humans learned how to communicate through writing.

Pictographs and Petroglyphs

The need to communicate complex ideas to others forced people thousands of yeas ago to invent written languages and numeric systems. The earliest forms of writing consisted of pictographs, symbols that expressed words or ideas. Many ancient examples of pictographs and petroglyphs—a pictograph drawn or carved on rock—exist today because they were carved on substances durable enough to survive for thousands of years, such as whale tusks, animal bones, animal skins, and tree bark.

Archaeologist Rodney S. Young has studied pictographs inscribed thirty-two thousand years ago on limestone walls in Turkey. He says the pictographs might look like aimless doodling, but they are important historical records of daily life in that long-ago era. He writes, "These drawings are the products not of specialists, but of common citizens; they reflect the contemporary scene, the things which the common man saw about him as he circulated every day. [They] are important sources for the life of the time—contemporary illustrations from a world long forgotten."[11]

Pictographs etched into stone are true to the earliest definition of *graffiti*, a term historians began using in the nineteenth century when they began studying the ancient images. *Graffiti* is actually the plural form of *graffito*, an English word derived from the Italian word *graffiao*, which means "scratched." Some pictographs are huge, like the Nazca Lines in Peru. The Nazca geoglyphs—the name for a pictograph carved into the ground—are more than twenty-five hundred years old. People of the Nazca culture made them by removing

reddish surface rock to reveal whitish ground underneath. The figures include artistic representations of monkeys, sharks, and llamas, and the largest are over 660 feet (201m) wide.

Over the centuries people invented alphabets so they could write words. Written language changed graffiti by allowing individuals to communicate advanced ideas with one another more easily than they could with symbols. Once written language was available, most graffiti was written rather than drawn or painted.

The Nazca geoglyphs, such as this spider, are pictographs carved into the ground. They have endured for thousands of years.

Written Graffiti

Some surviving samples of graffiti writing are more than two thousand years old. Written words found scratched on rocks and boulders in the desert of southern Syria, eastern Jordan, and northern Saudi Arabia date from about 100 B.C. They are historically important because they are the only existing remnants of Safaitic, an early form of Arabic writing. Ancient writings from Egypt, Greece, and the Roman Empire also have survived because they were etched or engraved into stone or wood.

The largest collection of ancient graffiti exists in Rome, Italy. More than a half-million examples of it were found in the Roman catacombs, underground burial places beneath Rome that were used mainly by early Christians. The messages etched into the catacomb walls between the fourth and seventh centuries include comments from a variety of writers, ranging from gladiators to young children. In 1863 archaeologist Giovanni Battista de Rossi claimed the graffiti was historically important because it showed the attitudes and ideas that people of that time held. He said,

> As we descended into the interior [of the catacombs] we are struck by the number of graffiti, as they are called, which cover the walls. [They are] rude scribblings of ancient visitors. [Many] valuable discoveries have been made by means of them and they have proved to be of immense importance, being the faithful echo of history.[12]

Archaeologists three decades earlier had found another valuable trove of graffiti when they excavated Pompeii, an Italian city that was buried under mountains of ash and cinder after the volcanic eruption of Mount Vesuvius in A.D. 79. The

Roman graffiti in Pompeii was preserved under volcanic ash. Written graffiti is sometimes the only remaining remnant of an ancient language.

volcanic debris preserved examples of written graffiti, such as *Lucius pinxit*, Latin for "Lucius painted this."

During the Middle Ages, from roughly the fifth to the sixteenth centuries, it was popular in England to engrave graffiti on churches. Many inscriptions were in Latin, and they often contained expressions of piety like this twelfth-century statement etched on St. Mary's Church in Walden: "My hope is in God because, O Christ, I trust in Thee." People used chisels or sharpened styluses to carve and scrape their remarks and sometimes added small drawings. Historian Violet Pritchard contends that people who created the flowing script of such messages and artwork were as skilled as any artists of their period. She notes that "owing to the constant cleaning and scraping of the stone surface [over centuries, some] graffiti only show the deeper part of the incision and much of their original beauty and craftsmanship has thus been lost."[13]

Not all graffiti from early times was artistic or expressed serious sentiments. According to historian Helen H. Tanzer, much of Pompeii's graffiti was commercial in nature and included advertisements for real estate. Many inscriptions from the once-buried town consist of juvenile humor, jokes about sex, and mindless ramblings about topics of no consequence. Tanzer calls this writing "mere scribbling resulting from *cacoethes scribendi* [Latin for an "irresistible urge to write"] which seems to have inflicted the infantile mind at all times and in all places since the beginning of writing."[14]

Gang Graffiti

Some of the most common twentieth-century graffiti in the United States has been done by street gangs in big cities. As early as the 1930s, Hispanic gangs in California were using graffiti to claim possession of neighborhoods. Gang graffiti has continued to flourish in inner-city areas of big cities across the country. According to art and graffiti historian Jack Stewart, gangs use the written form to threaten and intimidate other people. He writes, "[The graffiti] marked the boundaries of their turf; these warnings clearly came from the entire gang,

GANG GRAFFITI

One of the most prominent, early twentieth-century forms of written graffiti is gang graffiti. In the 1930s Hispanic gangs, sometimes called cholo gangs, began using it to mark their territories in Los Angeles and other California cities. This practice soon spread to gangs of all ethnic backgrounds throughout the United States. The Hispanic graffiti was called placas, Spanish for "plaques." Author Steve Grody explains:

Placas were declarations of territory and loyalty that emphasize the Neighborhood name first, followed by a "roll call" of gang members. Writing one's individual name alone was rare in this style, which was generally written in "Old English" or creatively angular derivations, emphasizing upper-case letters to convey prestige and serious intent. Variations of this cholo style, including Gang Block, sometimes done with three-dimensional edging, were seen around the city from the 1930s to the present day. Though no distinction may be made between gangs and graffiti crews in the public's mind, there is actually quite a bit of difference. Most graffiti writers limit illegal activities to painting. By contrast, gangs involved a much wider variety of crime and violence. Despite this, gang writing has made perhaps the greatest impact on L.A. Graffiti style, both in its letterforms and in the addition of roll calls to pieces, which are used almost universally by all graffiti crews today.

Steve Grody, *Graffiti L.A.: Street Styles and Art*. New York: Abrams, 2007, p. 12.

not just from the individual writer."[15] In Los Angeles, which has more gangs than any city in the world, such graffiti has been named "wallbangin'." Susan A. Phillips, who has studied Los Angeles gangs, explains, "*Wallbangin*' is a gang term that means, roughly, gangbangin' on a wall. This can be through straightforward writing or through crossing out the writing of others; either activity enforced relationships of power between gangs."[16]

Most gang graffiti is written simply, although Hispanic gangs will often write their name in an elaborate style of large letters which are referred to as *placas*—Spanish for "plaques"—which use an Old English style that has looped, pointed, and boxed or squared letters. Such graffiti often includes the name of the gang and its individual members along with gang symbols or numbers identifying the gang. Sotel gang members from West Los Angeles sign their graffiti "S, 1, 3," for Sotel 13. African American and Asian gangs use similar tags.

Members of a Los Angeles gang stand before a wall of gang graffiti that marks their territory in 1988.

Mindless Graffiti

Most written graffiti is not threatening; in fact, it is usually humorous or silly. An apparently disgruntled student once penned this inscription on a wall at the Harvard University library: "I've decided that to raise my grades I must lower my standards." And someone in a rest area off an interstate highway in Connecticut once wrote, "Of all the things I've lost, I miss my mind the most."[17]

The mindless nature of such graffiti is especially apparent in vulgar messages concerning sex, one of the most widespread forms of written and drawn graffiti through the ages. So many sexually-toned messages have been inscribed in public bathrooms that this graffiti genre has its own name—*latrinalia*. The term was coined in 1996 by Alan Dundes, a professor of folklore and anthropology at the University of California, Berkeley. Reisner describes the type of person who writes such graffiti: "There is the large group of second-hand exhibitionists, living in a world of sexual fantasy and getting their jollies from the imagined shock they are causing. [They are people] who enjoy nothing better than to violate a taboo. They flaunt their defiance by writing obscene words in public places."[18]

Another graffiti genre concerns modern music. One of the most famous examples of rock-and-roll graffiti was spray painted in 1967 on a subway station in London, England. It said, "Clapton is God," which refers to rock star Eric Clapton. Even though rock-and-roll singer Elvis Presley died in 1977, his fans still write graffiti messages to him on the wall surrounding Graceland, his home in Memphis, Tennessee. One message is written as if it were done by Elvis himself. It reads, "Please quit writin' on my wall. Thank you. Thank you very much. (E)."[19]

Travel Graffiti

People throughout recorded history have used graffiti as a way to mark where they have been. For example, when French soldiers invaded Egypt in 1798, they scrawled their names on the great pyramids of Egypt to prove they had visited the famous

ELVIS GRAFFITI

Graceland is the home rock-and-roll icon Elvis Presley lived in until he died on August 16, 1977. His Memphis, Tennessee, home is now a popular tourist attraction for his fans, and one way they honor him is by writing graffiti on a wall there. Author Daniel Wright explains:

W hile Elvis was alive, the groundskeepers did their best to keep the wall clean. After his death, however, the sheer volume of the graffiti proved overwhelming, and officials with the estate decided to leave the wall alone. Occasionally, somebody will write something crude or irrelevant, and Graceland hires a firm that uses high-pressure water equipment to clean the wall. Contrary to rumor, however, Graceland does not periodically sandblast the wall. It's the weather that does the damage to the graffiti; the sun and rain fade most messages within a year. Today, writing on the wall is as much a part of the Graceland experience as seeing the Jungle Room and the grave site. The wall is so long that you could spend hours reading from one end to the other. As you read, you'll likely see several tourists with markers in hand stopping to add their messages or have their snapshots taken next to a memorable piece of graffiti. Celebrities in town for a film or concert often pay tribute on the wall including rocker Billy Idol, who painted "Long live the King" in huge red letters.

Daniel Wright, *Dear Elvis: Graffiti from Graceland.* Memphis, TN: Mustang, 1996, pp. 38–39.

Elvis Presley's primary home, Graceland, contains a graffiti wall where fans can write notes in honor of him.

historical landmarks. The United States has an especially rich past in travel graffiti. For several hundred years explorers, fur trappers, and settlers moving westward across the continent left personalized messages of their passage.

El Morro National Monument in New Mexico contains some of the nation's oldest graffiti. *El Morro* is a Spanish name—in English it means "the headland"—because it was named by Spanish explorers like Juan de Oñate. Like hundreds of U.S. soldiers, miners, and settlers who would follow him, Oñate in 1605 signed his name on the huge sandstone wall and wrote, "pasa por aqui" (passed by here). In 1859 P. Gilmer Breckinridge chiseled his name into the same stone bluff after arriving with twenty-five camels in a failed U.S. Army experiment to use camels for desert travel. Other inscriptions on the bluff at El Morro include those of settlers moving west and workers who built the Union Pacific railroad in the 1860s. However, all of those visitors, including Oñate, were latecomers to the sandstone bluffs, which already had some drawings left hundreds of years earlier by Native Americans like the Anasazi.

In the nineteenth century Independence Rock near Casper, Wyoming, was a major stopping point along the Oregon Trail. Although it was named by a party of fur trappers who camped there on July 4, 1824, visitors who came afterward were proud enough that they had reached the famed landmark to carve their names in the large granite rock. Also in Wyoming is Signature Rock, a large sandstone cliff whose graffiti includes directions that helped guide settlers on a section of the trail discovered originally by mountain man Jim Bridger in the mid-nineteenth century. The Wyoming State Historic Preservation Office Web site claims the graffiti is historically important. It states, "The inscriptions indicate the route the trail took up the valley of Sage Creek. They are very significant because they substantiate the correct route of the Bridger Trail through an area with limited historic evidence concerning the trail route. The location and authenticity of the inscriptions has been confirmed."[20]

One of history's most famous examples of travel graffiti is a long-lasting World War II joke perpetrated by U.S. soldiers.

Independence Rock in Wyoming bears the graffiti of many travelers who have passed by it on their journeys.

HOBO GRAFFITI

In the twentieth century, hoboes were homeless people who often traveled from city to city by illegally catching rides on freight trains. Hoboes had a custom of leaving messages for each other that were written in a private language composed of symbols. These symbols warned other hoboes to avoid dangerous places or let them know where people would treat them kindly. For example, a rectangle with a circular dot meant danger and a circle enclosing an X meant that they could get some food at a nearby home. Author Robert George Reisner explains:

Although hoboes may have left their places of origin as individuals, they accepted and took care of each other in much the same spirit that members of a religious sect, ethnic group, or respectable fraternity will take care of each other. And the way they did it was through their graffiti. It was a highly imaginative, effectively functional written sign language, conveying important survival information such as the presence of vicious dogs, hostile police officers, areas where handouts could be expected, medical aid secured, or chain gangs existed. Chalked on backyard fences, doorsteps of houses, freight yard buildings, walls of public facilities, ashcans, [and buildings], a great many of the signs were around for [decades]. The graffiti of the hobo are the stationary expression of a mobile group.

Robert George Reisner, *Graffiti: Two Thousand Years of Wall Writing*. Chicago: Regnery, 1971, p. 79.

During the war, soldiers penned the phrase "Kilroy Was Here" everywhere they traveled. The scrawled phrase was often accompanied by a comical drawing of a face with a long nose hanging over what seemed to be a wall. One of the many theories for the origin of the graffiti is that a shipyard worker named James J. Kilroy wrote it on ships he inspected. Regardless of its origin, this graffiti became an iconic symbol of the U.S. soldiers who fought in that historic war.

Graffiti Survival

The fact that graffiti in the form of prehistoric cave art has survived for tens of thousands of years is heartening to a British graffiti artist known only as Banksy. One of the world's best-known graffiti artists, Banksy paid tribute to prehistoric graffiti by smuggling a fake rock painting into the British Museum in London in 2005. When his prank was discovered, Banksy issued this comment to the news media: "The only art to survive was made by those on the margins of society, driven into dank caves to paint. If our civilization was destroyed, future generations would piece together life in the 21st century using only the scrawlings on our subway walls."[21]

2

The Birth of
Modern Graffiti

Until the second half of the twentieth century, graffiti remained basically the same as it had been since primitive humans first began tracing and carving pictures on stone walls tens of thousands of years earlier. Art historian Jack Stewart says that the nature of graffiti had been static since its inception. He writes, "Worldwide, from ancient to modern times, the form and content of graffiti remained remarkably unchanged until the mid-1960s, when much larger-scale graffiti began appearing in Philadelphia, Pennsylvania. [The] graffiti that appeared in Philadelphia in the mid-1960s was different."[22]

The writing that began popping up all over Philadelphia was as different in style from the graffiti that had preceded it throughout the art's long history as were the tools artists used to make it—markers and spray paint. The artists' motivation for creating graffiti, though, was the same as it had always been—to make people notice and react to what they created. In the next few decades, this modern form of graffiti became a cultural phenomenon that spread across the globe, giving people a new form of artistic expression.

Graffiti's Philadelphia Roots

Philadelphia residents in the mid-1960s were already accustomed to gang graffiti, the symbols and names gangs scrawled in public places to mark their territory. But they were unprepared for the new graffiti that suddenly began appearing on walls, on the sides of buses and trolleys, and on just about any other surface that could be reached. The new graffiti was done in marker or spray paint that spelled out the artist's tag or street identity, and sometimes included a small drawing. So many tags appeared on the streets of Philadelphia that people began wondering who the taggers were and why they kept putting up these elaborate tags in so many different places.

One of the earliest Philadelphia tags was "Cornbread," which was boldly drawn with a swoosh at the end of the name and a small crown over the B. Many present and past graffiti artists have kept their real names secret, either because they shun publicity or are still afraid of being charged as criminals for their work. But Darryl McCray, who is considered one of the fathers of modern graffiti, has admitted he is Cornbread.

This artist tag was left by NOPE in 1995. Artists first began leaving their tag, or street identity, as graffiti in Philadelphia in the 1960s.

His tag comes from a nickname McCray earned in school for begging a cook to make cornbread, a food he loves. In 1965, when McCray was ten years old, he began writing "Cornbread" in his neighborhood to gain the attention of a girl he liked. He wrote, "Cornbread loves Cynthia" over and over, but his efforts failed when she moved away. In an interview with a newspaper decades later, McCray admitted that he kept writing graffiti after that because he enjoyed the notoriety it gave him. He says, "I was the only graffiti artist in the city of Philadelphia. For that matter, I was the only one in the world. The more people talked about Cornbread, the more I wrote it. I wrote my name all over South Philly [and eventually] people were really sick and tired of seeing my name."[23]

Other tags soon began showing up, like Cool Earl, Dr. Cool 1, Bobby Kidd, Sir Smooth, and Sherlock Holms. Cool Earl, who sometimes teamed with Cornbread to write graffiti, had a simple reason for what he did. "I started writing," he says, "to prove to people where I had been. You go somewhere and get your name up so people know you were there, that you weren't afraid."[24]

Graffiti artists made their tags famous by putting them in unusual spots. Bobby Kidd became legendary in Philadelphia for tagging a police car while a friend distracted its occupants. Cornbread became Philadelphia's most daring graffiti artist by tagging an elephant at the zoo and the Jackson 5's private jet when the popular singing group went to Philadelphia to perform. For the latter feat, McCray hid among Jackson 5 fans at Philadelphia International Airport. Amid the chaos fans caused when the group got off the plane, McCray sneaked away from the crowd and tagged the plane. Even though such acts are considered vandalism, McCray never felt he was doing anything terrible. "People [in gangs] got reputations for murdering people, stabbing people," McCray says. "I wanted a reputation as well, but I didn't want to hurt anybody for it."[25]

A few years after Cornbread became famous in Philadelphia, similar graffiti began appearing in New York City. And graffiti flourished there as it had never done before.

Julio 204 and TAKI 183

New Yorkers in the late 1960s began seeing "Julio 204" scrawled on buildings and in the underground subway system. Julio combined his nickname with the street he lived on—204th Street—to create one of the most famous early New York tags. Julio, though, never became as famous as TAKI 183, the graffiti artist whom historians claim was most responsible for igniting New York's modern graffiti craze.

In the summer of 1970, the sixteen-year-old high school student began writing on ice cream trucks near his home. His tag was composed of the diminutive form of his Greek first

TAKI 183

TAKI 183 became the most famous early graffiti artist because he wrote tags all over New York City so people with influence and political power would notice them. TAKI 183 explains:

When I was sixteen, my first job was as a delivery boy, and I used to make deliveries all over the east side [of New York]. That's what made me so popular. I used to write my name in areas where influential people would see it. Those guys who write for newspapers, they all live in nice neighborhoods. So they would see it and they said, "Au, God." But then they'd write about it the next day. If a guy like Junior 161 [an early African American writer from 161st Street] wrote his name up in Harlem, nobody [influential] would see it, only the people in that area. That's why I got the most publicity. I was in all the east side [subway] stations downtown. The main reason I started wasn't to publicize myself. In fact, maybe five people knew I was writing. The whole idea was to write and be with a group of people. They're all wondering who this guy is, but they don't know it is you, so you'd get a reaction from people. That was the whole idea.

Quoted in Jack Stewart, *Graffiti Kings: New York City Mass Transit Art of the 1970s.* New York: Melcher Media/Abrams, 2009, p. 23.

name, Demetrius, and the street he lived on in his Washington Heights neighborhood. Unlike previous graffiti artists like Julio who never strayed from their neighborhoods, Taki wrote his tag throughout the city. A job he had later as a messenger delivering packages helped him place his tag, "TAKI 183," in so many different places in the giant city that the *New York Times* ran a story about why he was doing it. Taki told a reporter who tracked him down that he began doing graffiti because he was bored. He said, "I didn't have a job then and you pass the time, you know. I took the form from JULIO 204, but he was doing it for a couple of years then and he was busted and stopped. I just did it everywhere I went. I still do, though not as much. You don't do it for the girls, they don't seem to care. You do it for yourself."[26]

In the *New York Times* story, Taki claimed police never arrested him for doing graffiti but admitted that he had been suspended from Harran High School for a day for writing on walls. He also said an agent for the U.S. Secret Service, the federal agency that guards government officials, sternly lectured him once for writing on a Secret Service car during a parade. The *Times* reporter did not use Taki's last name in the story to protect his identity, which is not known even today, but through his tag, Taki became a celebrity to millions of people.

The newspaper story said Taki's growing fame had already led to a flock of imitators. And Taki claimed the newspaper article caused another huge increase in the number of young people doing graffiti. "After a while it looked like they opened a faucet,"[27] Taki said years later.

The Graffiti Explosion

Graffiti continued to grow in other major cities during the 1970s, but New York became the epicenter for the most prestigious graffiti. Nicholas Ganz has written several books on modern graffiti. In *Graffiti World: Street Art from Five Continents*, Ganz explains why graffiti blossomed so strongly in New York:

> The unique make-up of New York City—in which the
> Harlem slums and the glamorous world of Broadway

stand side by side—seems to have been a breeding-ground for the first graffiti artists, bringing together many different cultures and classes in one single place. This environment fueled an artistic battle against the power brokers in society, and a breakaway from poverty and the ghetto.[28]

The amazing thing about the emergence of the new art form was that most graffiti artists came from inner-city neighborhoods plagued by social problems, such as poverty, a lack of education, and crime. Most artists were also Hispanic or black,

AN IMPORTANT NEW ART FORM

Graffiti historian Cedar Lewisohn believes the development of modern graffiti starting in the 1960s marked an important advancement in art. He writes,

In cultural terms, the [graffiti explosion] was a unique phenomenon. Its importance cannot be over-estimated. The phenomenon of dispossessed young people in New York City in the 1970s [who were] channeling their frustrations and boredom into making visual art—not music, not sport but art—is unprecedented. The art form they invented helped them to start to view the world in terms of all the visual languages that were available to them as sources to quote from and remix. We see this in piece after piece that happily steals from elements of pop culture. All of this activity happened completely spontaneously, with no initial financial backing or incentive, and the first group of graffiti writers had little or no art-school training or knowledge. This was a remarkable achievement, and it could be argued, the most culturally significant art movement of the second half of the twentieth century. No other movement since Cubism or Surrealism has developed such a distinctly new language.

Cedar Lewisohn, *Street Art: The Graffiti Revolution.* New York: Abrams, 2008, p. 31.

marking a strong contrast to the past when most well-known artists had been white, affluent, and educated. Mico, who is of Puerto Rican descent, was one of the early graffiti artists. Mico says he and other artists were motivated by a simple goal. He explains, "It began in different neighborhoods. But we all had one thing in common: We wanted to be famous. [It] was just about getting up [a tag], getting around. The more hits [tags] you had, the more famous you became."[29]

Such fame was important to young people from impoverished backgrounds who often had few hopes for a bright future. Herbert Kohl was a New York teacher who tutored Johnny Rodriguez, a thirteen-year-old Puerto Rican youth who had dropped out of school because he could barely read and write. Kohl became intrigued with graffiti when he noticed that the youth was scribbling "Bolita" on the elevator doors and halls of his apartment building when he came for lessons. Kohl learned that Bolita—Spanish for "little ball"—was the nickname his mother had given the teenager. Rodriguez stopped writing in Kohl's building when Kohl asked him to stop. But when Kohl began seeing "Bolita as Johnny Cool" and other similar tags near his apartment building, he knew Rodriguez had written them. Kohl noticed that when he saw Rodriguez on the street, he seemed to be more confident and outgoing than the shy, uncertain young man he was during lessons. Kohl attributed that to the psychological boost the youth got from seeing his tag in public. He explains, "Johnny appeared in a different perspective to me [on the street] because of the way he was described on the wall. [He] seemed like another person on the streets—or perhaps it would be more appropriate to say that he was another person with me during lessons."[30]

The ego boost Rodriguez got from becoming known for his tag is a major reason so many people write graffiti. That same psychological need for recognition among their peers also led graffiti artists to quit writing their names in simple letters. In their attempts to be the best, they began creating bigger and more elaborate tags, and their work eventually became a visual art phenomenon.

Some kids, who might otherwise be shy, gain confidence from seeing their tags displayed on the streets.

Graffiti Evolves

The earliest graffiti tags were done in marker, and they were fairly small and had simple lettering. Mico says competition among artists changed that. He explains, "The letters got more refined and larger and larger. We were each trying to outdo the other."[31] The easiest way to make tags more dramatic was to use paint cans powered by aerosol spray instead of markers. Graffiti historian Jon Naar says the move to spray paint radically altered graffiti. He explains, "[The art] was detonated by the newly introduced technology of the spray can as a quick way to write messages in color on walls and other flat surfaces."[32]

Aerosol cans quickly became the graffiti artist's tool of choice and changed graffiti forever; graffiti today is sometimes called "aerosol art." Spray cans not only brought vibrant color to graffiti but also allowed graffiti artists to make their works bigger and do them faster because the cans release paint so quickly. It took artists a long time, however, to learn to control the spray, to use it to shape letters, to shade and color background, and to make everything fit together as an artistic whole.

Graffiti also became more elaborate as writers—the name they prefer to *artists*—began using creative letter styles to make their tags more interesting. A style called Broadway elegant has long, thin, closely packed letters, and Brooklyn style has free-flowing letters decorated with hearts, arrows, and curlicues. Bubble style features fat letters that are often oddly shaped and outlined with a different color. Geographers David Ley and Roman Cybriwsky say that the highly styled lettering makes the tags mini works of art. They explain, "The signature is distinctive. It is usually spray-painted from an aerosol can and is highly accentuated, embellished with elegant curves and generous serifs. The letters, like the name itself, convey a message of 'style.'"[33]

The most creative new lettering is Wildstyle, a complex form that incorporates interwoven and overlapping letters and shapes and can include decorative elements like arrows, hearts, clouds, and spikes. Wildstyle lettering is so intricate it is hard

A graffiti artist spray paints his art onto a wall. Graffiti tags were initially done in marker, but spray paint allowed colorful messages to be written more quickly.

WHERE THE ARTISTS LIVE

The Faith of Graffiti, *published in 1974, was the first book that treated modern graffiti seriously as art. The book features hundreds of pictures of graffiti by photographers Jon Naar and Mervyn Kurlansky with several pages of text by famed novelist Norman Mailer. Naar, in a book he authored himself years later, claims that people could not understand 1970s graffiti without knowing where the artists lived. He writes,*

*A*s you read the street numbers on the tags and in photographs [you] will see that the vast majority of the writers came from the most-run-down and neglected sections of New York: Harlem, Washington Heights, the Bronx, and the Lower East Side. The writers, like the other inhabitants of those districts at that time, were predominantly Hispanic and African-American. The graffiti they sprayed on the fronts of homes [and] on the trains that ran through their neighborhoods were a cry for change from the ghetto to clean up the filthy streets, to improve the quality of the schools, and to reduce the glaring inequities between rich and poor. Via the trains and buses the writers sent their message to more affluent parts of the city as well as leaving their marks on (mostly) public spaces.

Jon Naar, *The Birth of Graffiti*. New York: Prestel, 2007, p. 19.

for people not familiar with it to read it. Historian Henry Chalfant says no one artist developed Wildstyle, but he credits a graffiti writer known as Phase 2 with having a major influence on it. Chalfant declares, "He's definitely one of the fathers of it. His wild-style lettering is very important."[34] Chalfant describes Wildstyle as a fluid form, one that makes the words it spells out come alive for everyone who sees it.

Graffiti styles evolved rapidly in just a few years even though the artists had to invent them as they were doing it. Eric Haze, who began doing graffiti in 1973 and today is a graphic designer, describes its early development: "There was still no blueprint [so artists with] a few cans of paint combined with their desire for self expression created what [is] perhaps the only other truly American art form born [in the twentieth century] in the wake of jazz."[35]

The ultimate goal of artists who pioneered modern graffiti was to be noticed—and they achieved that quickly by the sheer volume of what they wrote.

Graffiti Everywhere

There were two ways early graffiti artists earned recognition from their peers as "kings," or masters of the art: by putting up a huge number of tags or by placing them in hard-to-get spots. Putting a tag on a wall, subway car, or other surface is referred to as "getting up" or "getting around" and a tag is called a "hit." If a prolific writer writes hundreds of tags in one area, it is called "killing" or "bombing." Artist Japan 1 notes, "You have to put in the hours to add up the names. You have to get your name around." Some artists, like Junior, dislike the artier styles because they take longer to do. He says, "That's just fanciness. How're you going to get your name around doing all that fancy stuff?"[36]

Some artists enjoy the challenge of targets that are hard to hit because they are in places that are always crowded or where security is tight. Michelle, one of the rare women graffiti artists, gained fame in 1972 by tagging the Statue of Liberty on Ellis Island in New York. And in 1976 Kap, who called himself "the Bicentennial Kid," tagged the Liberty Bell in Philadelphia two weeks before the July 4th celebration of the nation's two hundredth birthday. Kap died of leukemia that November, but his hit earned him everlasting fame. Cay 161 also enjoyed difficult tags. His most famous was on a well-known New York City fountain. Cay explains how he did it: "I wrote my name with white spray paint on the wing of the angel

Graffiti marks a subway car's window in New York City. Putting a tag on a subway or on other difficult sites is a way to get your name known.

in Bethesda Fountain and a lot of people said, 'Wow, how did he get up there and do that?' I grabbed one of the wings and climbed up."[37]

The news media began calling the work the artists did graffiti, but the writers themselves reject the term. Mico says the word *graffiti* is as vile to him as a racial or ethnic insult. He explains, "The term 'graffiti' is to 'writing' what the 'N' word is to African Americans and what the 's' word is to Puerto Ricans."[38] Writers hate the term because they prefer to be known by their own names and because they do not want anyone else defining what they do and who they are.

By whatever name, more and more people, most of them young and poor, were drawn to graffiti. By the early 1970s so many people were tagging every available blank public space that it began to be difficult to find room to write more tags. One of the most popular places to tag had been the inside of subway cars but, as space filled up, people began writing on the outside of the cars. And in the 1970s, New York's subway cars became the backdrop for some of the wildest, most brazen, and most artistic graffiti ever produced.

3

Graffiti's Golden Age

A rt historians consider the mid-1970s to the late 1980s to be the golden age of graffiti. One of the leading graffiti artists of the time was Leonard Hilton McGurr in New York, whose tag was Futura 2000. During this period, McGurr saw graffiti transformed from simple tags done in marker to complex works of spray paint art. McGurr says, "If you look at graffiti in New York in the early 70s, it was whack [not cool], it was very crude. I'm speaking unholy words—because we're talking about the Mecca [of graffiti]—but it took us time to work out what we were doing, since we were inventing as we went along."[39]

McGurr's abstract and artistic designs influenced the more complex lettering that helped graffiti grow and change from stylized writing into a full-fledged art form. A major factor in this evolution was that graffiti artists began working on much bigger spaces, which allowed them to let their imaginations and their creativity expand onto the huge surfaces they covered. Although some artists still used blank walls and other public spaces, the most daring and creative made the exteriors of subway cars their canvas of choice. They did this because they knew the cars would make their tags famous by allowing millions of people to see their work as they moved through the giant city.

Subway cars are 75 feet (23m) long and 12 feet (3.7m) high. Tags consisting of brightly colored, twisting letters and whimsical figures often ran the length of a car, and a few were several cars long. The speed with which the cars flashed by people in subway stations made the mobile art works look even more amazing than when the cars were standing still. Claes Oldenburg, one of the twentieth century's most honored sculptors, loves the spray-painted cars. Oldenburg believes the cars added a needed touch of color to the city. He says,

> I've always wanted to put a steel band with dancing girls in the subways and send it all over the city. It would slide into a station without your expecting it. It's almost like that now. You're standing there in the station, everything is gray and gloomy and all of a sudden one of those graffiti trains slides in and brightens the place like a big bouquet [of flowers].[40]

This detail from a graffiti wall was created by several early artists, including a group of artists known as the Fabulous Five. The Fab 5 were active in New York City during the golden age of graffiti.

Like other graffiti, what became known as subway art is illegal. However, the possibility of being arrested by police or security guards was only one of the hazards artists faced during this period while creating technicolor spectacles that transformed New York City.

Subway Art Dangers

To paint New York subway cars, artists had to climb or cut fences to enter holdings yards and layups, the aboveground areas where extra cars are stored on weekends and during non-rush hours when there are not as many riders. These areas are at the ends of the lines in areas like the Bronx, Queens, and Brooklyn. The work was usually done at night, which meant the mostly teenage artists had to sneak away from home and brave the dangers of New York's crime-ridden city streets to find a car to paint.

Lee Quiñones, who was born in Puerto Rico and grew up in New York, began painting subway cars in 1975 when he was fifteen years old. Before he stopped writing graffiti a decade later to create paintings and other more traditional art, Quiñones had made his tag, "Lee," one of the era's most famous. Among his accomplishments was painting an estimated 115 whole subway cars. And in November 1976, he and five other artists known as the Fabulous Five managed the seemingly impossible feat of covering all ten cars in one train from top to bottom with colorful graffiti—the only time one group painted an entire train. Quiñones is proud of the art he created, but years later he admitted it had been dangerous. He recalls:

> My mother feared for my life, 'cause I was leaving home in the middle of the night and coming back in the early morning, when I was supposed to be going to school that day—but I wasn't. [At] any given time, I could've met death. Whenever I finished painting a train, I would christen it by giving it a kiss—wet paint and all, say, "Good luck," and then I'd smack it.[41]

Graffiti artist Lee Quiñones is known for painting an estimated 115 subway cars as a teen—which he admits was dangerous work.

Some graffiti writers did come to harm. In the book *The Faith of Graffiti*, author Norman Mailer notes that one young man was killed beneath a subway car while painting it and another was seriously burned when a paint can caught fire from a spark. One danger was that the subway cars sat on three rails that included one with live current to propel them when needed. Mico says the teen writers ignored such dangers to paint graffiti. He explains, "When you're young, you don't really realize the danger you're putting your behind in. You don't realize that you're dealing with 600 volts of electricity [and that] people have gotten killed."[42] But Japan 1 admits, "I was scared all the time I did it."[43]

Artists often had to flee from police officers and transit authority guards who would arrest or even brutalize them. During the winter of 1973, Cliff 159 and two friends were in the Gun Hill Road station when the police caught them with cans of spray paint. Cliff 159 says, "The cop picked up the can [and] started spraying in my face, but the can wouldn't work [because it was frozen]. I slipped away from him and ran onto the tracks [and escaped]."[44] On September 15, 1983, twenty-five-year-old Michael Stewart died after transit authority guards beat him for spray painting graffiti in a Manhattan subway station.

Writers kept coming back despite the dangers, and according to graffiti artist Stag 161, they were usually free to do their painting:

> We would write out in the open. Citizens were intimidated to the point where they would not say anything. We had free reign over the yards and lay-ups. Yes, there were token arrests, but while one guy was being escorted out the south side of the tunnel, there would be three or four more writers on the north side still carrying on with their craft.[45]

For many, the risks seemed well worth it. Sandra Fabara, who made the tag "Lady Pink" famous, was one of the few female subway writers. Fabara, who grew up in New York but was born in Ecuador, began painting cars when she was fifteen. "I was already famous as soon as I started, just because I was a girl,"[46] says Fabara. Graffiti's illegality and attendant dangers kept many women away from it. However, those factors are what drew Fabara. She says, "I was attracted to the adventure, the rebelliousness of it. The more guys said, 'You can't do it,' the more I wanted to do it. It was the risk of it, but also having fun, to be cool and popular."[47] Fabara showed males she was worthy of joining them by ignoring danger and working hard to become a good artist.

In contrast to most arts, part of the skill of graffiti writing is the ability artists need to avoid the dangers involved in doing their art. In the 1980s Alain Maridueña tagged subway cars as Ket One. Maridueña continued creating graffiti and studying it around the world even after the subway era ended. In 2009 he stated, "Train writing was and is a movement that involved skill, stealth and heart."[48] The artists needed to develop skills, such as locating a subway car to paint and evading authorities long enough to finish their work, just to do the art they loved.

Subway Graffiti Style

When graffiti's golden era began in the 1970s, artists simply wrote their names on subway cars in larger letters than they had used inside the same cars. But because they had more time in the deserted storage areas, they were able to create complex, unique tags that took up so much space they began calling them "pieces," a term that is short for "masterpiece." Artists also invented new terms for other, even grander works—a "panel piece" was graffiti painted below the windows and between the doors of a subway car while "block buster" was a wide-lettered graffiti style that stretched the length of a car. Steven Ogburn, a writer who is credited with inventing the latter style, explains why he began writing his tag, "Blade," so big: "I wanted to make sure you could see a train from five blocks away and you could read it. COMET 1 and myself invented the blockbuster [style] in 1980: very large, square words, but very legible. We painted over five thousand trains each, over the span of those years."[49]

STEVE OGBURN

Steve Ogburn (Blade) was one of the most prolific New York subway artists in the 1970s and 1980s. In a 1999 interview, he talked about graffiti's golden era:

I got started painting trains back in 1972. Lots of my friends were painting. It was just simple hits, what they call tagging now—we all got into it at that time for fun, just to be crazy kids. There were people before me, but I was one of the first people doing an actual "masterpiece" on a train. When I began writing, people didn't know how to make a piece [masterpiece] at all. There was nothing on the trains, just scribble. I did five thousand train [cars] between 1972 and 1984. I did it on the trains for the danger, the rush of being out in the middle of the night in the train tunnels and the train yards. It was a Huck Finn–Tom Sawyer type of a life—every day was a real adventure! Back then, putting up your name was the general idea of graf [graffiti]. When you went to the trains years ago, it was about bombing and seeing your name going from every borough in the city and tens of thousands of people know who you are. It was great! It was like this huge party going on for a decade and a half.

Quoted in James Prigoff and Robin J. Dunitz, *Walls of Heritage, Walls of Pride: African American Murals.* Rohnert Park, CA: Pomegranate Communications, 2000, p. 141.

Even though aerosol cans enabled people to write tags more quickly, it took subway artists a long time to cover an entire car. Super Kool 223, who is credited by some historians with having created the first graffiti masterpiece, discovered that spray nozzles from consumer products like oven cleaner could be transplanted onto paint cans to produce a wider spray. The innovation was called a "fat cap," and it helped artists do their work even more quickly. But using a "fat cap," or any spray can for that matter, is not easy. Graffiti historian Jack Stewart explains how difficult it is to learn spray-can technique: "It is extremely hard to keep spray paint from dripping when spraying on a vertical surface, and even respected artists occasionally had trouble with it. From the beginning, dripping paint was the most obvious mark of a toy."[50]

Learning to control the spray was only a small part of the education of a "toy," the term for a beginner or someone who was not very good. Serious graffiti artists had many other techniques to master, such as how to overlap letters creatively while still leaving them readable and how to give letters a 3-D effect through the use of complex shading. In addition to fat caps, artists used

Graffiti artists put the finishing touches on their 3-D artwork, a technique artists began to use in the 1980s.

GRAFFITI VOCABULARY

All-CITY: A term used in New York City referring to a graffiti artist or crew that has placed its work throughout the city's five boroughs.

BITE: To copy another writer's style.

BLOCK BUSTER: A graffito with wide letters that extends from end to end on a subway car below the level of the car's window.

BOMB: When a writer creates so many graffiti works that his work is noticed because of its quantity.

BUFF: The term for when graffiti is removed.

BURN: When a writer or crew beats fellow writers to tag an area.

CAPS: A cap is a nozzle on a spray paint can; they can be either fat or skinny depending on the size of the spray the cap produces.

CREW: A group of writers who band together to create graffiti; another term for *crew* is "clique."

CROSSING OUT: When somone adds something to another writer's work, crosses it out, or defaces it. Such acts show disrespect to the original artist.

FADE: When an artist blends colors.

GETTING UP: When artists are noticed because they have so many signed graffiti.

GETTING OVER: When an artist is able to place graffiti in many places.

HIT: A generic term for any graffiti piece.

KILL: When one area is covered excessively with graffiti.

KING: A graffiti artist considered the best in the style he works in.

PANEL PIECE: A painting on a subway car that is below the car's windows and between the doors of the car.

PIECE: A large, well-done graffiti, stemming from the word *masterpiece*.

PIECE BOOK OR BLACK BOOK: The name for the book in which artists sketch their works and the works of other artists.

PRODUCTION: A very large mural that has detailed artwork.

RACKING OR RACKING UP: Another term for shoplifting; some writers steal their paint supplies, either because they are poor or they think it's cool.

TAG: As a noun it refers to the name a graffiti artist signs on his work; as a verb it means to create a piece of graffiti on any surface.

THROW-UP: A graffiti work that has to be done speedily so the artist is not caught doing it.

TOY: Nickname for a new writer or one whose work is not very good.

WRITER: Anyone who creates graffiti.

other caps that produced fine sprays so they could outline their work or create details like arrows and hearts. Artists also began adding abstract shapes and caricatures of people and animals to their tags. They even borrowed characters from popular culture, like Donkey Kong, Nintendo's early video game. In 1983 Son 1 and Rem painted a Mario Brothers–like figure on a train in Manhattan, New York. There were also nude figures occasionally, usually female, but officials usually painted over them quickly.

Full-car creations were the most impressive. In 1980 Ogburn drew his tag name across a subway car in black, fat, squiggly letters against a pink and red background. The tag looked menacing and its letters, outlined and shaded in white and gray, appeared three-dimensional. In 1980 Donald J. White, one of the most famous and most respected subway writers, covered a car from top to bottom with fat, tilted letters spelling out his tag—"Dondi." Done on a light-blue background, the letters were shaded in several colors, including pink and green, and his tag was flanked at either end by waiflike figures that added a touch of humor. Works of all sizes and in every shade imaginable adorned the cars, and most had stylistic quirks that gave them a unique look. Some lettering was so stylized as to be nearly unreadable, but that did not detract from the exotic effect the colorfully painted cars created as they pulled into subway stations.

Most subway artists were dedicated to producing their creations and took great pride in them. But those feelings were bittersweet because many people who saw the graffiti considered it vandalism and not art. Quiñones says that his subway art "rolled in its own private subterranean stage [the subway], which consisted of one of the world's largest audiences, but who never even noticed its life."[51] Even sadder for Quiñones than having his art ignored was the fact that, like other subway artists, he never knew when his creations would be wiped away by public officials.

Graffiti Is Not Forever

Museums around the world have statues, paintings, and even some examples of graffiti that are thousands of years old. But the artists who transformed New York's subway system into a rapidly moving art exhibit knew their work might not survive even one week. In addition to public officials who would buff out or paint over their work, they also had to contend with other graffiti artists who might alter or deface their art. Tracy 168, a legendary artist of this period, was especially upset when officials wiped out work he did in 1976, the year the United States celebrated its two-hundredth birthday. He says, "I wrote GOD BLESS AMERICA for the bicentennial. I did three pieces in red, white, and blue, and it was so beautiful that the MTA [Metropolitan Transportation Authority] immediately painted over it. They couldn't let anyone know that [graffiti artists] loved America."[52]

Due to the diligence of authorities, the work of graffiti artists often existed for only a short time. However, some subway art has survived in photographs. Martha Cooper and Henry Chalfant took pictures of graffiti for years and eventually published their pictures in 1984 in the book *Subway Art*, one of the period's most important historical records. Chalfant became friends with the artists, who would alert him to new pieces they wanted him to photograph. Chalfant would have to figure out where and when the car would run on the subway lines and then wait in the proper station to take its picture. Chalfant writes, "I was always working against time since I could never be sure if a piece would remain intact for very long. Somebody might cross it out or the Transit [officials] could 'buff' [erase] it. I felt like I was stalking rare big game when I went out to take pictures of graffiti."[53]

As graffiti began to clutter buildings and subway cars, a large segment of the public became opposed to it. Many people did not appreciate the art. Others rejected it because it was vandalism of private property or were angry about the cost of cleaning it up. A 1972 *New York Times* editorial titled "Scratch the Graffiti," a clever take-off on the original meaning of *graffiti*, states, "The graffiti are no longer amusing; they have become a public menace."[54]

Starting in the early 1970s, city officials like New York mayor John Lindsay began fighting to wipe out graffiti. In addition to a

DOCUMENTING SUBWAY ART

The book Subway Art *is a collection of pictures taken in the 1970s and 1980s by Martha Cooper and Henry Chalfant. It is a revered historical source of graffiti from that era. Cooper became interested in graffiti while working as a photographer for the* New York Post. *In the twenty-fifth anniversary edition of the book, published in 2009, Cooper says she was introduced to graffiti after taking a picture of a young boy flying pigeons, who then talked to her about his graffiti. Cooper writes,*

He showed me his notebook of drawings and said, "Why don't you photograph graffiti?" He explained that he was sketching his nickname, "HE3," and showed me how he had painted it on a wall. This was a revelation! I finally understood that graffiti was mostly kids writing their names. I thought, "Wow! These kids are designers!" Because I expressed so much interest in graffiti, HE3 offered to introduce me to a "King," who turned out to be Dondi [Donald J. White]. By luck, Dondi had clipped one of my photos from the Post that happened to have one of his pieces in the background and pasted it in the front of his black book. The photo had a credit line so he recognized my name." [He] taught me graffiti terminology and introduced me to other writers. The more I learned about the culture, the more I wanted to photograph it.

Martha Cooper and Henry Chalfant, *Subway Art*, 25th Anniversary ed. San Francisco: Chronicle, 2009, p. 6.

campaign to erase painted trains and increase subway security, New York passed a law banning the sale of spray paint to minors. The efforts failed to stem the rising tide of graffiti. The paint ban was ineffectual because most artists preferred to steal their paint, and those who purchased it did so in other communities. And

A volunteer paints over graffiti on a mailbox in New York City. The city began a crackdown on graffiti in the early 1980s, which led to a drastic decrease in subway art.

New York was struggling so much financially in that period that it did not have enough money to stop the artists.

According to Chalfant, the graffiti crackdown failed at first because it accented the art's illegal nature, which made it more fun and challenging for artists. Eventually, however, the cleanup crusade took its toll on artists. Chalfant writes, "I would say by '83, '84, there were really good artists dropping out. They'd work and work, and their stuff wouldn't run [on subway lines] or it would get crossed out by some jerk."[55]

The end came in 1989 when New York City finally had enough money to increase subway security and keep artists out of storage areas. Security measures included patrolling the areas with dogs. The city also began taking painted cars out of service immediately, which dismayed artists so much that they quit.

Even though graffiti artists continued working on walls and other public spaces, the demise of subway art ended what many consider to have been graffiti's greatest period of creativity.

"Watching My Name Go By"

Super Kool was one of the artists who turned New York's subway system into an exotic mobile art show. Although not everyone appreciated their work, he and his fellow artists loved watching their subway art rush by them. In 1974 he said, "I sometimes go on Sunday to the Seventh Avenue and 6th Street station and just spend my whole day watching my name go by."[56]

Social and Political Graffiti

In April 2008 the words "One Nation Under CCTV" mysteriously appeared in wide, white letters on the faded tan wall of a post office building in London. At the bottom of the three-story message, whose words were centered neatly under one another, were two figures—a young boy clad in red wielding a long-handled roller brush and a security guard watching the graffiti artist paint. Above and to the right of the graffito was a cluster of real security cameras overlooking a fenced-in, supposedly secure area that included the wall. The news media credited the audacious work to Banksy, whose politically oriented works have made him one of the world's most famous graffiti artists, even though his real identity has never been proven. A London newspaper once claimed that Banksy is an Englishman named Robin Gunningham, but Banksy has never admitted his true identity.

Banksy's graffiti was a commentary on how little privacy people have in a high-tech world in which officials can use cameras to spy on people committing criminal offenses, such as writing graffiti. The work created a sensation because Banksy had erected scaffolding three stories high to create his graffito even though security cameras were monitoring his every action. Banksy believes artists have the right to create graffiti in public places to make political comments. He says,

> Bus stops are far more interesting and useful places to have art than in museums. Graffiti has more chance of meaning something or changing stuff than anything indoors. Graffiti has been used to start revolutions, stop wars, and generally is the voice of people who aren't listened to. [And] even if you don't come up with a picture to cure world poverty you can make somebody smile.[57]

People for thousands of years have used graffiti in the form of written slogans, drawn or painted images, and combinations of the two methods to comment on political and social issues. Messages delivered in graffiti have run the full gamut of beliefs people have held in all times and places. And as Banksy shrewdly notes, unauthorized messages written in public spaces have often been the only way some people could make such comments.

Graffiti by the British artist Banksy depicts British soldiers in riot gear chasing a girl holding a soccer ball. Banksy's graffiti often makes political statements.

Political Graffiti

Painting words on blank walls is a cheap and easy way to make a political statement. Authors Robert Reisner and Lorraine Wechsler believe that this is why the poorest and most humble people in any society have adopted this method through the ages to vent their anger and frustration or their support or opposition to various political issues. They also contend that political graffiti can provide unique insights into the history of the periods in which they are written. Reisner and Wechsler write, "Graffiti are the voice of the common man. We are used to taking our history from aristocrats and statesmen and their paid scribes [public relations people]. But through graffiti we discovered evidence of another version of history, characterized by oppression and opposition to the official point of view."[58]

The oldest remnants of political graffiti date back thousands of years. Graffiti historian Cedar Lewisohn writes that graffiti in ancient Rome "was a popular way of speaking back to authority. The city walls constituted a place where people could ridicule, or complain about, the authorities."[59] At times throughout history, though, people who used graffiti to criticize those in power were punished for it. When Nero was emperor of the Roman Empire (A.D. 54–68), for example, he imprisoned and even killed people who wrote negative graffiti about him.

Perhaps the most famous—and certainly the largest—example of political graffiti was that on the Berlin Wall, a structure that from 1961 until 1989 divided Communist East Germany from democratic West Germany. The wall was 15 feet (4.6m) tall and more than 100 miles (161km) long, and East Germany erected it to prevent citizens from fleeing Communist rule. When it was dismantled in 1989, the entire length of the western side of the wall was covered with graffiti. Historian Hermann Waldenburg describes the many types of graffiti found on the Berlin Wall: "There were wise sayings, inanities, daydreams enciphered in human figures, faces, skeletons, landscapes, animals [all combining to become] the world's longest painting."[60]

The most compelling topic among the messages written on the Berlin Wall was political freedom, such as the bold decla-

A man takes part in the destruction of the Berlin Wall in 1989. Stretching more than 100 miles, the Berlin Wall was the largest example of political graffiti.

ration "COMMUNISM STOP!" Famed New York graffiti artist Keith Haring contributed a 325-foot-long (99m) mural of figures that appeared to be stretching themselves so thin that they could get under the wall and escape to freedom. An even longer, though somewhat cryptic, political statement was made by a former East German who used a paint roller to draw a continuous chest-high, white line along the wall for 6 miles (9.7km). Stopped when border guards arrested him, the artist was sentenced to six months in jail.

Political graffiti is still popular today, especially in Latin American countries where widespread poverty makes it difficult for many people to voice their opinions any other way. In the book *graffiti brasil*, authors Tristan Manco, Lost Art, and Caleb Neelon explain that officials in cities in Brazil make it easy for people to create political graffiti. They write, "Before an election, the city is whitewashed, primarily to impress the

BRETT COOK

As Dizney, Brett Cook has created mural-size works of graffiti that comment sharply on social issues. In 1984 when Cook was sixteen years old, he spray painted a wall in San Diego, California, that pictured two black crayons with stylized tall afro haircuts struggling over a lighter-colored crayon. The 10-foot-high (3m) graffito included this question: "Why Fight for A Crayon That's Not Our Color?" Cook, an African American, later became a successful commercial artist. He explained years later that the graffito was a commentary on the struggle blacks have in their daily lives in dealing with values of the dominant white majority that may differ from those African Americans hold. He said,

T his piece was about some of the struggles and challenges that African Americans were facing, and continue to face, within their own culture, oftentimes related to compromising their [racial] identity for success or achievement. Two African American young men with haircuts and clothing of the era are pulling on a crayon, trying to have ownership of a good idea or a representation that is clearly different from themselves. [The] worst part about us African Americans isn't that we have to fight our ethnicity to be adopted by society. The worst part is that it is often other black Americans that we fight with. Why are we so inclined to fight for a crayon that is not our color anyway?

Quoted in James Prigoff and Robin J. Dunitz, *Walls of Heritage, Walls of Pride: African American Murals.* Rohnert Park, CA: Pomegranate Communications, 2000, p. 173.

electorate [about the city's cleanliness], but also to provide a blank canvas for new election murals."[61] The newly blank spaces also give nonpolitical graffiti artists new chances to practice their art.

Political parties and elected officials who wield authority have also used graffiti to influence public opinion. In fact, one of the most powerful and historic uses of graffiti for political purposes was the way the Nazi Party employed it to win control of Germany and persecute Jewish citizens.

World War II Graffiti

German dictator Adolf Hitler wrote *Mein Kampf*—its title in English means "My Struggle"—while he was imprisoned in 1924 for treason due to his failed attempt to take over local government in Munich, Germany, a move that was supposed to have been his first step in seizing power in Germany. Published after his release from prison in 1925, the book was a blueprint for gaining political power. In it Hitler explains how his National Socialist (Nazi) Party could use propaganda to win political support. He cautions that propaganda—ideas or statements designed to influence other people's beliefs—should be simply worded so anyone could understand its message. He writes, "Propaganda must always be presented in a popular form and must fix its intellectual level so as not to be above the heads of the least intellectual of those to whom it is directed. The art of propaganda consists precisely in being able to awaken the imagination of the public through an appeal to their feelings."[62]

Hitler's skillful use of propaganda helped him win political control in Germany less than a decade later in 1933. Nazi propaganda appealed to people emotionally rather than intellectually.

Anti-Jewish slogans mark a shop in 1938 Germany. Graffiti became a tool the Nazis used to spread their propaganda.

Hitler's powerful speeches were peppered with short, dramatic phrases such as "Deutschland über alles" (Germany over everyone), and Nazi public rallies were dramatic, entertaining events filled with loud music and colorful, waving flags that excited people. Hitler also chose the swastika as the party's main symbol. The bold, intimidating crooked-cross figure was universally recognized and created instant identification for the party wherever it appeared.

Graffiti fit neatly into Hitler's vision of what propaganda should be because it is good at expressing short, simple messages. His followers employed it profusely to spread Nazi beliefs. Using paint, chalk, and other substances, they scrawled phrases from his speeches on public spaces throughout Germany. The Nazis also used graffiti to attack political opponents and Jews. The menacing swastika often accompanied graffiti propaganda or was drawn alone as a symbol of the party's growing power.

Much of Nazi propaganda was anti-Semitic. In his speeches, Hitler blamed Jews for Germany's defeat in World War I and for current economic problems. Hitler knew this tactic would be popular because anti-Semitism had always been strong in Germany. Nazis scrawled, "THE JEW IS OUR GREATEST ENEMY, BEWARE OF THE JEW" and other graffiti on Jewish businesses and synagogues, and the swastika became the world's most powerful anti-Semitic symbol. Graffiti also played a role in Hitler's attempt in the late 1930s to take legal rights away from Jews and persecute them so they would leave Germany. Jewish journalist Bella Fromm says that in 1938 in Berlin, where she lived, "everywhere were revolting and bloodthirsty pictures of Jews being hanged, tortured, and maimed, accompanied by obscene inscriptions."[63]

Graffiti was also a weapon for people who opposed Hitler. During World War II, which Hitler started in 1939 by invading Poland, it was dangerous to criticize the Nazis. But in 1942 a group of University of Munich students called the White Rose began circulating leaflets attacking the war and Hitler. The group and its supporters used graffiti in this campaign by

THE WHITE ROSE

During World War II, a group known as the White Rose distributed leaflets criticizing Nazi rule in Germany. The group was led by Hans Scholl and his sister, Sophie, who were college students. Members of the White Rose also used graffiti to attack Nazi leader Adolf Hitler. On the night of February 3, 1943, group members wrote, "Freedom" and "Down with Hitler" on the walls of Munich University and other buildings. In his book An Honourable Defeat: A History of German Resistance to Hitler, 1933–1945, *author Anton Gill describes what happened the next day:*

The following morning [members of the White Rose] went to the university to attend a lecture. On a wall by the entrance the word "Freedom" had been written in huge letters. . . . A large group of people were watching a handful of Russian women laborers trying to clean it off. "They'll have a hard job," said Sophie. "That's bituminous [tar-based] paint." Another friend, Traute Lafrenz, who was one of the leaders of the Hamburg White Rose [was] in Munich too that day and saw Hans Scholl. "I remember he was smiling to himself. Some outraged student or other came up to him and said, 'Have you seen what's happened?' 'No,' said Hans. 'What?' But his smile broadened. From that moment on I began to be terribly afraid for him."

Two weeks later Hans and Sophie were arrested with leaflets in their possession. They were found guilty of treason and beheaded on February 22, 1943.

Anton Gill, *An Honourable Defeat: A History of German Resistance to Hitler, 1933–1945.* New York: Holt, 1994, p. 190.

writing phrases like "HITLER THE MASS MURDERER!" and "FREIHEIT" (freedom) in large letters on streets and buildings throughout Germany.

Although the Nazi Party was destroyed when Germany lost World War II, the swastika survived as a powerful anti-Semitic symbol. In fact, it has become the most all-purpose graffiti symbol of hatred and is used to demean people worldwide on the basis of race or religion.

Hate Graffiti

In April 2009 Orlando Diaz and his family returned from a vacation to find the interior of their Phoenix, Arizona, home covered with swastikas and other Nazi graffiti, as well as KKK emblems. KKK stands for the Ku Klux Klan, a racist group that has persecuted blacks for 150 years. On January 22, 2010, someone scrawled swastikas on the Kenesset Israel Torah Center in Sacramento, California. Simone Clay, president of Kenesset Israel, says, "It's very sad to see it's still happening."[64] Just a few weeks later in France, swastikas were painted on a Muslim mosque. On February 1, 2010, swastika symbols and the letters KKK were discovered on doors and windows at Belleview High School in Belleview, Florida; their target was African American students.

Incidents in the United States that involve such graffiti are considered hate crimes, criminal offenses in which bias against a person or group because of race, religion, sexual orientation, or ethnicity is the reason the perpetrator committed the act. The federal government and most states have separate hate crime laws with stiff penalties for such acts. Hate graffiti is one of the most common hate crimes, which also include other forms of vandalism, arson, verbal or physical assault, and murder. Thousands of graffiti hate crimes are committed each year in the United States against people on the basis of race, color, religion, national origin, gender, disability, or sexual orientation.

A lot of hate graffiti is written by teenagers like the nine who, in January and February 2010, spray painted swastikas, racial slurs, and obscenities on property in Bourne and Sand-

The following text appears within the image (graffiti on the wall):

المركز الاسلامي
THE ISLAMIC CENTER
OF AMERICA

GO
(RAH)
YOU IDOL HOME 91
WORSHIP

wich, Massachusetts. Bourne police lieutenant Richard Tavares says the graffiti was probably not motivated by hate: "We think they were just looking for attention. And unfortunately, now they're going to get it."[65] Although some graffiti is undoubtedly due to juvenile pranks rather than hate, graffiti experts warn that hate graffiti should be taken seriously because it can be an early warning sign that the writers may act physically against the targets of their graffiti.

In the 1970s, geographers David Ley and Roman Cybriwsky studied racist graffiti in Philadelphia that had been written on buildings near streets that were borders between black and white neighborhoods. They determined that the presence of graffiti like "WHITE POWER" and other racist phrases was linked to violence against blacks in newly integrated areas. Their study showed that some racist incidents in

Vandals applied hate graffiti to the Islamic Center of America in Dearborn, Michigan. Hate graffiti, one of the most common hate crimes, is a criminal offense.

areas that had a lot of graffiti were so severe that blacks fled the neighborhoods. Ley and Cybriwsky write, "Graffiti might be regarded as a rather whimsical element, [but] the quality and location of graffiti manifest [indicate] the distribution of various social attitudes [and] certain types of graffiti forecast both potential and actual behavior. To borrow a current graffito: 'Today's graffiti are tomorrow's headlines.'"[66]

The connection that exists between graffiti and possible physical harm to people it targets was behind the federal investigation of more than two hundred hate crimes against African American Barack Obama after he was elected president of the United States on November 4, 2008. Many anti-Obama hate incidents involved graffiti, including, for example, some race-tinged phrases four college students in Raleigh, North Carolina, sprayed in a pedestrian tunnel. The U.S. Secret Service, which guards the president, investigated the graffiti to make sure it would not lead to violence against Obama. Special Agent Darrin Blackford of the Secret Service says, "We're trying to be out there at the cutting edge of this [to protect Obama]."[67]

Hate graffiti of all types can be found in every part of the world. Also global in scope is antiwar graffiti like that generated by the Iraq War.

Antiwar Graffiti

People have used graffiti to oppose war in almost every period of history. During the Vietnam War in the 1960s, the phrase "Make love, not war" could be found scrawled on the walls of every big city in the United States. But the Iraq War, which began in 2003, inspired more graffiti than any conflict in history. This was due to graffiti's popularity around the world by this time and to the opposition to the war that existed in many countries. Xavier A. Tàpies wrote the text for a book of photographs of anti–Iraq War graffiti from many countries. He says graffiti gave antiwar activists an opportunity to state their views exactly as they wanted. Tàpies writes, "[Graffiti] suddenly became one of the few uncensored channels of expression in an almost fascistic political climate. [A] brilliant bunch of artists used hyper-eloquent graffiti to give voice to the sense of fury [that many people] felt at runaway government. [Graffiti] claimed its place as the visceral medium for real political expression."[68]

Written graffiti included messages like "war is naughty," which was spray painted in Brighton, England, and the words "NO WAR" that appeared in black paint on the winglike shells of the Sydney Opera House, one of Australia's most famous buildings. The opera house's chief executive, Norman Gillespie, criticized the people who sprayed their message on the revered building. He stated, "While we respect the right of

Antiwar protestors spray painted the words "NO WAR" on the Sydney Opera House in Australia.

Mohammed Ali is an unlikely graffiti artist. He was born in Bangladesh but grew up in Birmingham, England. Ali, who is known as Aerosol Arabic, uses graffiti to show people that not all Muslims are terrorists like the ones who attacked the United States on September 11, 2001. In his blog Ali writes,

Traditional art never interested me. Learning about Van Gogh's life wasn't particularly inspiring for me. Graffiti became a big part of my life, almost an obsession. It was during my early twenties when I began to rediscover my faith. Questioning what life was all about, and where I was heading. Discovering Islamic calligraphy, and the fascinating parallels with graffiti. . . . As a graffiti artist I already had an obsession with the written word, so it was fascinating to discover how Islamic art was focused primarily on the written word, but instead of man's word, it was the word of God, written in intricate, elegant and fluid styles. . . . I became drawn to Islam, this was my solace. It gave me meaning, and Islam was now a big part of my life. Then September 11th happened. By this time I was experimenting with Islamic calligraphy and graffiti art. The two passions in my life were melded together, expressing my identity as an urban Muslim born and raised in the west.

Mohammed Ali, "Spiritual Graffiti in the USA, an Emotional Rollercoaster Ride," aerosolarabic: urban islamic art (blog), http://aerosolarabic.wordpress.com/2007/04/30/the-usa-tour-summary-an-emotional-roller-coaster-ride.

Mohammed Ali, known as Aerosol Arabic, used his graffiti to try to show people that not all Muslims are extremists.

Australians to protest, it was a totally unacceptable way of doing it. To deface such a wonderful icon was an act of reckless vandalism, totally unacceptable."[69] The protest forced the opera house to institute new, twenty-four-hour security measures.

A lot of antiwar graffiti was much more artistic than mere writing. In Amsterdam, the Netherlands, a graffiti artist known as PJ spray painted "Make Jokes Not War" in English on a wall. The pink, orange, and blue bubble-style letters reminiscent of the golden age of graffiti appeared to float on blue and green clouds with a small black-and-white peace sign to one side. In Buenos Aires, Argentina, a replica of the Statue of Liberty with a skull face and holding a sickle instead of a torch depicted the U.S. symbol of freedom as the grim reaper of death. The art was done with a stencil, a newer graffiti method that enables artists to work quickly to avoid being arrested.

A favorite target of the antiwar graffiti was U.S. president George W. Bush, whom many people around the world blamed for starting the conflict by ordering the invasion of Iraq. Graffiti included Bush wearing a football helmet while clutching a bomb instead of a football in Cambridge, Massachusetts, and "BUSH" written in fat letters over a picture of a skull and crossbones in Rome, Italy. Anti-Bush graffiti was found in at least twenty-six countries.

There was also graffiti supporting the Iraq War. In Boston, Massachusetts, someone wrote "GOD BLESS BUSH USA" near graffiti calling Bush a murderer. And in 2005, someone who was allegedly a U.S. soldier wrote on a bathroom wall in Fallujah, Iraq: "Enjoy your freedom? Thank an American Marine!"

Mohammed Ali, an artist from Birmingham, England, who combines Muslim calligraphy with modern graffiti, tries to lessen the prejudice against Muslims that was caused by the Muslim terrorists who attacked the United States on September 11, 2001. Ali, who is known around the world as Aerosol Arabic, visited several U.S. cities in 2007, including New York, where he spray painted wall graffiti honoring nine children and an adult who died in a house fire. His classic-style graffiti includes a verse from the Koran—"Verily To God We Belong . . . TO HIM WE

SHALL RETURN"—and the names of the victims. Creating the work profoundly affected Ali. He says, "Today changed me. Today I truly tasted the fruits of what art can bring. All I could hear was them [family and friends of victims] weeping behind me. This is spiritual, taking graffiti to the next level, reaching out to the community. Not just this community, but Muslims and Christians and Jews. This is something really powerful."[70]

5

How Modern Graffiti Spread

Beijing residents were puzzled in 1995 when spray-painted images of a bald head with a prominent chin began turning up on buildings in the capital of the People's Republic of China. In the next three years, more than two thousand of the bizarre images appeared to further confuse people who had never seen this modern type of graffiti. Zhang Dali, a graduate of Beijing's Central Academy of Fine Arts, brought graffiti home to China after seeing it in Italy. Graffiti since then has slowly spread to other Chinese cities like Guangzhou, where Sic, a native of the city, founded Made in Guangzhou, China's first graffiti crew. Sic loved graffiti so much after seeing it on the Internet that she had to create her own. She explains, "It was crazy! You could do it anywhere. It wasn't necessarily beautiful but it was daring and brave."[71]

To many people the fact that graffiti was still alive and well in the twenty-first century was amazing, especially in a nation like China, which was culturally isolated from current global trends for much of the twentieth century and whose government still frowns on many types of individual expression. In fact, most people had believed the graffiti craze would die out in 1989 after New York officials were finally able to secure the

71

city's subway cars, which had been the most dramatic and visible examples of the new art. But that did not stop graffiti artists from pursuing their art elsewhere. In a far-sighted statement about graffiti, Maze 139 boldly declared, "We may have lost the trains . . . but we've gained the whole world."[72] It was not long before his prophecy was fulfilled. Modern graffiti soon began to travel the globe from its New York birthplace, and it became an accepted part of many different cultures in countries far different from the United States, like China and Israel.

Graffiti Goes Global

One of the early catalysts that helped spread graffiti globally was the book *Subway Art*, published in 1984. It features photographs of graffiti taken by Henry Chalfant and Martha Cooper. When Cooper visited Europe in 2003, many graffiti artists told her *Subway Art* had inspired them to start doing graffiti. "My favorite," Cooper recalls, "was the English writer who playfully shook his finger at me and said, 'You have a lot to account for.'"[73]

Graffiti got a giant global boost from hip-hop, the music and dance craze that became popular in many countries during the last two decades of the twentieth century. Graffiti became a major element of hip-hop culture because both developed about the same time in the 1970s in poor areas of New York and other big cities. When hip-hop culture spread around the world, so did graffiti. Clifford Joseph Price, who is of Jamaican and Scottish ancestry, discovered graffiti in England in the 1980s through his involvement in hip-hop music. Price says, "If I didn't learn graffiti the way I did—letter forms and outlines —I don't think I could do music the way I do now. It wouldn't be the same."[74] Price is famous today as Goldie for both his graffiti and his music.

In 1983 *Wild Style*, the first hip-hop movie, glamorized graffiti by featuring legendary subway writers Lee Quiñones (Lee), Donald J. White (Dondi), and Sandra Fabara (Lady Pink). Graffiti also began showing up in the backgrounds of

CLIFFORD JOSEPH PRICE

As Goldie, Clifford Joseph Price gained fame as both a graffiti artist and a hip-hop musician (and later as an electronica and drum and bass artist). Because modern graffiti and hip-hop both began during the 1970s in big cities like New York, the cultures of the two new crazes became intermixed. Thus when hip-hop became popular in other countries, so did graffiti. Price explains how he was first drawn to graffiti and how it has developed since then:

I felt compelled when I first saw graffiti [in the 1980s]. It was large, it was beautiful, it said everything that I wanted to do. It was something that I could express myself with, in a way that I never thought I could. So you're inspired to be part of something you don't really understand. . . . If you think about something like the bubble letter, just a letter with an outline—graffiti, in its beginning—that's like thinking about a club that only has one record deck. It's very hard to go back and think about how it evolved. A graffiti writer learns his skill in fonts and function. Graffiti, in its purest essence, is exploring the letter form. There are purists who explore the letter form alone. They adapted a simple language, the alphabet, and manipulated it, backwards, forwards, inside out, twisted it and took it to another level.

Quoted in Cedar Lewisohn, *Street Art: The Graffiti Revolution.* New York: Abrams, 2008, p. 44.

movies and television shows like *Welcome Back, Kotter*, a comedy about a high school teacher in a poor area of New York. English graffiti artist Mode 2 says that seeing graffiti in street scenes in the opening shots of *Kotter* made him want to learn more about it. Scottish graffiti artist Lyken Love—his tag, not his real name—also fell in love with graffiti the first time he saw it in 1983. He explains, "Weirdly, the first graffiti I ever saw was in six foot high skinny letters spelling out the words 'The Philadelphia Kids' and, even stranger than that, was the fact I was in Durban, South Africa at the time!"[75] Within a few years Lyken Love was writing graffiti in his native Dundee, Scotland.

A major factor in graffiti's growth was the development of the World Wide Web. In the 1990s graffiti Web sites became a powerful tool in introducing millions of people to the art form. New artists have gotten started doing graffiti just by trying to imitate work they have seen on the Internet.

Today graffiti exists in every corner of the world, although it is called by different names in other languages, such as *ktvot kir* (writings on the wall) in Hebrew, *rakugaki* (writing where it is not allowed) in Japanese, *pichação* (to trace or stain) in Portuguese, and *tu yo* (scribblings without purpose) in Mandarin Chinese.

The most important factor in the spread of graffiti around the world has been the willingness of graffiti artists to share their knowledge with newcomers. This camaraderie has strengthened graffiti from the time New York teenagers began painting subway cars every color of the rainbow in the 1970s.

Graffiti artist Goldie, right, and his crew pose with their artwork. Hip-hop culture and graffiti developed around the same time.

THE GLOBAL GRAFFITI SCENE

The book Graffiti Planet 2: More of the Best Graffiti from Around the World, *published in 2009, features a collection of graffiti from around the world collected by Alain Maridueña, a graffiti artist with the tag "Ket," who is famous for his 1980s subway art. In his book Maridueña describes the global graffiti scene. He writes,*

Walking the Streets of Berlin, São Paulo, Paris, and the Bronx [New York], it is easy to see that the aerosol art and writing movement is alive, well, and consistently growing. In such places there are [several] distinct schools of thought amongst graffiti artists. Some favor "bombing"—in other words the sport of tagging, which is all about getting our name around town quickly and prolifically. Another school, specifically in Berlin [Germany], has gone for an "anti-style" approach, where the names are created in simple designs reminiscent of New York, circa 1973. Another development has been the growth of the "street art" phenomenon, either where writers have turned to art that avoids the traditional use of letters, or art school students have decided that they too want to be part of the excitement of being public outlaws with their work.

Ket, *Graffiti Planet 2: More of the Best Graffiti from Around the World.* London: O'Mara, 2009, p. 1.

Camaraderie and Goodwill

During graffiti's golden age, graffiti artists were friendly to one another even though they were competing to write the most tags or produce the biggest, most dramatic pieces. One reason for the closeness was that graffiti artists had common enemies—police and security guards who would arrest them for what they loved doing. They often shared information about law enforcement activity aimed at stopping them. Mico explains, "Especially in the beginning, it was a guerrilla war. We had strategic maps of the subway system, of which yard or layup was hot or cooled off. We gathered intelligence. And if you got chased out at Coney Island that morning, you came to the bench and told everyone it was hot."[76]

Graffiti artists gathered to share information, exchange techniques, or simply socialize at gathering spots they called either a "writer's bench" or "writer's corner." Some of their most popular meeting places were subway stations like the West 168th Street Station because the artists could watch their work travel past them while they talked. Skilled artists also shared their expertise with newcomers in one-on-one sessions, everything from spray-painting techniques to how to evade security to get into layups and yards housing subway cars. This educational process included becoming a member of a crew, a group of artists who worked together to produce graffiti under one tag. This was important to graffiti's growth. Fabara explains, "We're not taught [something like this] in school, this is nothing formal in a book or anything. It's all taught word of mouth, handed down master to apprentice. The only way to learn any of this stuff is to take up with a master or just somebody that knows a little bit more than you do and have them teach you the ropes."[77]

That sense of camaraderie helped thousands of people in New York join the graffiti explosion in the 1970s and 1980s. That sense of fellowship also existed after modern graffiti made its way to California in the mid-1980s. Fear and Dove, who began writing graffiti several years after its arrival in Los Angeles, found that established artists were happy to help them. "When Dove and I met respected writers," Fear says, "they were cool with us and would teach us things." Artists also helped each other develop their skills. Fear explains, "I schooled Dove a bit, but then he started excelling and learning different things that I never learned, so he started to school me a little bit. We learned from each other. [He] might learn some of the new tricks that people were doing and he'd get them down before I would, then I'd ask him 'How the hell did you do that?'"[78]

Despite the overall level of goodwill among graffiti artists, there was some jealousy and competition. Individual artists and crews would stage graffiti battles on the same wall to see who could produce the best work. Leonard Hilton McGurr (Futura 2000), one of the famed New York subway artists, admits that graffiti artists sometimes wrote over or defaced the work of rival artists. "I think we all have [experienced that]," McGurr says. "But that's part of the history and tradition of the culture, for better or worse [some artists] will always provoke negative responses."[79]

That same sense of camaraderie among graffiti artists in New York also helped spread graffiti to other countries. When U.S. graffiti artists visited foreign countries, they were happy to

Sandra Fabara, known as Lady Pink, poses in 1996 before one of her murals in New York City.

GRAFFITI CREWS

Graffiti crews have often helped inexperienced artists learn to do graffiti. Educator Richard S. Christen explains:

The first crews were master groups of highly skilled and experienced writers. . . . The high standards and exclusivity of these crews created intense competition among those vying for membership as well as between rival groups. Beginners' crews and groups composed of writers at various levels of proficiency also surfaced. The Baltimore writer Deka became involved in one of these multi-level crews as a teen. Touched by "a fever" for graffiti at the age of ten, he regularly cut his high school classes to watch and draw with older, more accomplished writers who would critique his work and at times share letter models with him. Eventually some took him into their crew, where Deka assisted on pieces designed and executed by his mentors: "They took me on, and I just started doing characters and stuff like that cause they were doing heavy detail work," he recalls. "Its almost like an apprenticeship, they'd start you off with characters so you couldn't mess up the wall too bad."

Richard S. Christen, "Hip Hop Learning: Graffiti as an Educator of Urban Teenagers," *Educational Foundations*, Fall 2003, p. 57.

introduce people to their art. And that is one of the main reasons Brazil has become one of the most important centers of graffiti.

Brazilian Graffiti

In 1978 artist John Howard moved to Brazil, the only Latin American country in which the official language is Portuguese instead of Spanish. Brazil already had a lasting tradition of *pichação*, the country's name for written political graffiti, but Howard introduced artists like Rui Amaral to modern graffiti.

An even more important visitor was Barry McGee, who went to Brazil in 1993. McGee had created formal artwork to earn a degree in painting and printmaking from the San Francisco Art Institute, but he had also painted graffiti as Twist. His graffiti is distinguished by a trademark character, a male figure with sagging eyes and expressions reminiscent of the transients and other homeless people who inhabit San Francisco streets.

McGee worked with many Brazilian artists, including nineteen-year-old twin brothers Otavio and Gustavo Pandolfo. Today they are world famous as Os Gêmeos—Portuguese for "the twins"—and they credit McGee with shaping their graffiti careers. They say, "Twist made an important visit to São Paulo in 1993. We learned so much from him, and the information exchange was very important to [our] work."[80] The twins, who live in São Paulo, were also tutored by graffiti artists from other countries, including Zekis, Doze TC5, Jonone156, and Loomit.

Brazil has a tradition of written political graffiti, or *pichação*, which in the late 1970s became influenced by modern graffiti styles. This mural in Rio de Janeiro depicts a politician and a young person.

Their involvement in break dancing and hip-hop music had already led the Pandolfo brothers to begin doing graffiti in the late 1980s. Even before McGee's visit, they were writing their tag with latex paint, which is the most common graffiti medium in Brazil because it is cheaper than spray paint. But with the help of foreign graffiti artists, the twins developed their graffiti talents and became known for complex pieces that usually included one or more of their trademark yellow-skinned people. In paying tribute to subway art graffiti, they once painted a railroad car with one of their yellow-skinned characters lying down and extending the length of the car. Their one-time tutor McGee lavishes praise on their graffiti. He says, "Their work ranges from lyrical and touching portraits of their beloved family to the gut-wrenching images of São Paulo's homeless, crippled, and forgotten. The brothers also mine Brazilian folktales, literature, and their own mutual family and world of fantasy for source material."[81]

When the brothers are interviewed, they give united answers to questions because they consider Os Gêmeos to be a single art entity. "We are both part of one world: our world,"[82] they told one reporter. In his book *Graffiti World: Street Art from Five Continents*, author Nicholas Ganz credits the twins' fantastic imagination with their production of some of today's most interesting graffiti. He writes, "Their pictures are reminiscent of drawings and illustrations from children's books and are plastered in every possible—and impossible—place."[83]

Ganz believes the mural-like works Os Gêmeos have created in Brazil and other countries have stretched the boundaries of graffiti in new directions. Os Gêmeos claim their graffiti evolved differently from graffiti in other countries because they knew so little about the art when they started. "We never watched anyone else painting [so] we tried to discover how these things were done," they say. "We think we ended up discovering other things as a result."[84]

Brazilian culture undoubtedly shaped the way the brothers did their graffiti. Cultural differences have also shaped graffiti in other countries, and as a result, graffiti is a little bit different wherever one travels.

Graffiti Evolves Around the World

Dali said he began drawing those strange bald heads in Beijing in 1995 because "graffiti is a quick but extremely powerful way of communicating with people. I started doing it because I wanted to communicate with the city."[85] However, because Communist officials tightly control individual expression in China, graffiti has grown slowly there. Chinese artists are not free to criticize their government. Beijing graffiti artist Seker notes, "There can't be political themes, and if there are, they must be beneficial towards the government or the [Communist] party."[86] That contrasts sharply with graffiti in countries where artists are free to criticize political figures and issues like war and poverty.

Cultures of various countries have even led to new forms of graffiti. Brazil is famous for innovating *grapixo*, a hybrid form of graffiti lettering. This graffiti blends the thin, angular letters of São Paulo's *pichação*, which covers almost every bare space of every building, with the colorful, artistic lettering of modern graffiti that originated in New York. As such, *grapixo* reflects *antropfagia*, a Portuguese term for cannibalism that in Brazilian art means to borrow things from other cultures and adapt them to Brazilian culture.

Graffiti historian Cedar Lewisohn writes that such changes are to be expected because "the worlds of graffiti writing [are] constantly reinventing themselves."[87] This artistic evolution is happening not only due to cultural differences in various countries but also because of new media that artists are using today. They include stencils, which are figures, shapes, and letters cut out of paper, cardboard, or other materials that allow artists to spray paint their work on various surfaces.

Graffiti artists began using stencils because they speeded up their work, which helped them avoid being arrested. Famed English graffiti artist Banksy says that when he was eighteen years old, police nearly caught him while he was painting "LATE AGAIN" in silver bubble letters on a passenger train.

Banksy says he got the idea for using stencils while hiding from police under a dump truck for over an hour, with oil from the truck dripping on him the whole time. He explains, "As I lay there listening to the cops on the tracks, I realized I had to cut my painting time in half or give up altogether. I was staring straight up at the stenciled plate on the bottom of a fuel tank when I realized I could just copy that style and make each letter three-feet high."[88]

Stencils helped Banksy become famous. He decorated walls, bridges, and other flat surfaces in cities around the world with bizarre images of monkeys carrying weapons of mass destruction, policemen with smiley faces, and rats wielding drills and umbrellas.

Banksy, however, was only following in the footsteps of an earlier stencil graffiti artist from Paris—Blek le Rat, who was born in Paris in 1952 as Xavier Prou. Prou became famous in the early 1980s and acquired his tag for stenciling images of rats all over the city. Prou says he chose rats as a political statement. He explains, "They are the rebels of the city. They are evil. They live in groups. They steal food from the supermarkets. And Paris is full of rats. So it was a way of saying [be] careful where you're living."[89] Prou was influenced to pursue his graffiti career by the "Kilroy Was Here" messages U.S. soldiers had written during World War II, which were still present in Paris when Prou was growing up. He also saw examples of modern graffiti when he visited New York in 1971. Prou's work often involves political messages, but his stenciled images of people are so artfully done that they seem to come alive on the walls on which he places them.

The Lonely Graffiti Artist

Although graffiti has spread to nearly every nation in the world, it struggles to survive in many countries. A1one is one of only a few graffiti artists in Iran, a country in which such Western forms of culture are frowned on by a government dominated by Islamic religious leaders. A1one is also Iran's most famous artist, and he has exhibited his stencil graffiti in

Shown here is a self-portrait of stencil graffiti artist Xavier Prou, known as Blek le Rat. Prou became famous for stenciling images of rats around Paris.

A man paints over graffiti displaying campaign slogans in Iran in 2009. There are few graffiti artists in Iran, where the government strongly discourages Western forms of culture.

the United States. Even though A1one is almost the only one doing graffiti in Tehran, Iran's capital, he is encouraging and helping other budding artists. In a 2008 interview, he said,

> So, yeah in one way I am alone doing my work, but in another way there are about 30 younger artists around, checking my blogs, emailing me questions, doing graffiti. I even suggested to some of them to start using Farsi [the language in Iran] and some of them are. I really have hopes about the future of these guys. I hope the next generation will be better and [they] may "bomb" the city someday. Maybe !!!![90]

6

Graffiti—Art or Vandalism?

Barry McGee's paintings sell for thousands of dollars and have been shown at prestigious galleries, like the San Francisco Museum of Modern Art. Many of his other artworks, graffiti pieces signed with his street tag, Twist, have appeared on walls, trains, and other flat surfaces around the world. In 2001 when McGee was in New York City to appear on a television show about modern art, the San Francisco artist admitted he had written graffiti during his visit. McGee was amused at the wildly different reactions people have to his graffiti and his more traditional art. He says, "It [my graffiti] just looks like all other graffiti in New York that everyone hates. [But] at the same time I'll walk three blocks and be inside the gallery and be doing what I do with the same hand and people are saying, 'Oh, art, this is great, this is so superb, I love this stuff.' [I] like that; that's funny to me."[91]

McGee's gallery and museum art includes paintings and installations, works he creates by using different types of materials, objects, and media to transform a blank space into something artistic. His installations, which are often political statements on urban problems like poverty, addiction, and the homeless, can include images painted on walls and other objects such as liquor bottles purchased from street people. McGee may even scatter broken glass and punch a few holes in walls for added effect. McGee makes a living from such art but cares more about graffiti he does for free. He explains, "Every time I do a gallery piece, I have to put 110 percent more outdoors, to keep the street cred. It's the audience I'm most concerned with."[92]

Like many graffiti artists, McGee feels the pull of two worlds: the art world, which accepts his graffiti as art, and the general public, which sees it as vandalism.

Graffiti artist Barry McGee, who uses various materials in his art, displays his work in art galleries.

FIGHTING GRAFFITI WITH GRAFFITI

City officials have used many different methods to fight graffiti, from low-tech, chain-link fences to high-tech, graffiti-seeking intelligence services that utilize digital cameras and global positioning system (GPS) to find and analyze graffiti. But the strangest tool used to fight graffiti has to be graffiti itself. In Los Angeles, businesspeople like Alberto Sanchez hire graffiti artists like Edward Mompeller (Playboy Eddie) to paint graffiti murals on their buildings. Sanchez owns Chico's Mexican Restaurant. He would rather have murals Mompeller paints, which depict Latino history or a positive message for the community, than gang tags and obscenities. Sanchez claims the murals have helped keep negative graffiti off his walls because Mompeller is so respected by other graffiti writers that they leave his work alone.

This new tactic to curb unwelcome graffiti has even spread to foreign countries. In 2009 officials in Chesterton, England, set aside space in their subway system and encouraged young artists to paint whatever they wanted in an attempt to avoid having more negative graffiti placed there. Also in 2009 a nonprofit group in Montreal, Canada, hired graffiti artist Guillaume Lapointe to paint murals on buildings in the city's Notre Dame de Grâce neighborhood, including the Snowdon Bakery. Owner Abie Gmora said he is much happier having a baker wearing a white hat and some colorful abstract figures on his wall than scribbled tags that disfigure his business and have no connection to it.

Graffiti and Vandalism

In 1972 the *New York Times* editorialized that "subway graffiti are fast reaching what [a city official] has called 'the epidemic stage' here."[93] Since then many cities in the United States have passed laws making graffiti illegal and making it harder for graffiti artists to obtain the materials they use to create graffiti, such as spray paint. Regardless of how creative or beautiful a graffiti piece might be, it is typically placed on someone else's property without the permission of the owner. While many people may not have an objection to the art itself and some may even appreciate it, many do not think that it is right that graffiti artists create their work in places that do not belong to them.

In 1990 Lompoc, California, passed its first antigraffiti law to make it unlawful to deface property by graffiti, to sell spray paint to a minor, or for anyone younger than eighteen to purchase or possess spray paint. But two decades later, graffiti was still a problem there. In February 2010 Lompoc resident David Grill complained about graffiti near River Park. "Over the past two months," Grill said, "it's been quite ferocious. It [is] overwhelming."[94] Graffiti is considered a problem worldwide, even in places like the remote South Pacific islands of Fiji. In 2009 town administrator Vijay Chand complained about obscene graffiti painted on walls. "It is a menace in this town and we are trying to create awareness on the need for more civic pride,"[95] Chand said. Many people still hate graffiti and try to stop it because it is a crime to write on property someone else owns and much of it, like gang tags, is ugly and intimidating.

Some artists today paint legally on spaces provided by local governments or businesses or on media like canvas so they can sell their work. However, many artists still enjoy the bandit aspect of graffiti that has always attracted so many people—the adrenaline rush artists get by doing something illegal without getting caught. As Chinese graffiti artist Sic coyly admits, "Some people prefer doing the legal stuff. It's more obedient but I like it out on the streets. I guess my heart's not yet at ease."[96] The love of doing something illicit is so strong that some graffiti writers have said they would quit if graffiti were legalized.

Graffiti is not only considered an unwanted nuisance by many people but is also expensive to clean up. Ironically, some famous graffiti artists have become victims of graffiti. Taki, whose "TAKI 183" tag helped popularize graffiti in the 1960s, admitted in a 1989 newspaper story that the business he

A man who vandalized a statue in Brazil with graffiti is made to clean it up.

owned had been tagged repeatedly. He accepted the graffiti philosophically: "I am a victim. I painted it over and two weeks later it was all written up again. But I guess what goes around, comes around. It's justice."[97] In another irony the company founded by Edward Seymour, who invented canned spray paint, today markets a product to remove graffiti.

However, the graffiti that most people hate is graffiti that has no artistic merit, like gang tags, messages expressing religious or racial hatred, and obscenities. In an August 11, 2009, editorial about the need for tougher law enforcement to curb graffiti, the *Milwaukee Journal Sentinel* stated, "Most graffiti isn't art, it's just vandalism."[98]

Graffiti as Art

When complex spray-painted tags and subway aerosol masterpieces appeared in New York during the 1970s, many art critics, teachers, and other people who appreciated traditional arts, like painting and sculpture, dismissed graffiti as colorful acts of vandalism. But graffiti had its defenders even then.

In 1975 Hugo Martinez organized United Graffiti Artists so artists could display their work at a gallery. The exhibition drew a rave review for its "purity" from Peter Schjeldahl, one of New York's most influential art critics. The "purity" Schjeldahl praised was that the graffiti was created by people with no art training, which means that it is original and untainted by previous conceptions of what art should be. Also in 1975 English art critic Lawrence Alloway wrote about graffiti in *The Nation*, a prestigious magazine about politics and culture. Alloway admitted he enjoyed graffiti's "marks of individualism," "primitive energy," and the bright colors with which the pieces were done. He even commented positively on graffiti's illegal nature: "Though the writing amounted technically to vandalism, it's hard to object to the brilliant floralization of complete trains."[99]

In the 1970s many critics and art teachers were not very accepting of modern graffiti because it did not fit their definition of what art should be. In the decades since then, though, that definition has expanded to include graffiti along with other,

JUAN TAPIA-MENDOZA

As C.A.T.-87, he wrote graffiti. As a doctor, he treats sick children. But even as a doctor, Juan Tapia-Mendoza has remained attached to graffiti. In 2004 he and three other physicians opened Pediatrics 2000, a clinic in New York that provides emergency medical care for children at night. Tapia-Mendoza allowed Hugo Martinez to open an art gallery in the $2 million clinic and hired graffiti artists like Tracy 168 to decorate some of the clinic's walls. Tapia-Mendoza recalls,

Graffiti made me feel important. I became somebody. I was admired, respected and feared because of that mysterious air that accompanied the early writers. I was able to focus on one goal. Before that I had no goal in life, I lived every day as it came. I learned how to set goals like hitting all one-hundred buses in a depot in one night or hitting every Number 1 train station from South Ferry to 14th Street in a couple of hours. By focusing, I was able to set higher goals like starting to read one book, passing my GED [general equivalency diploma], then on to college and medical school. It made me feel important in front of the people that meant something to me. It showed me how to set goals for myself, especially short-term goals, and gave me a feeling of accomplishment.

Quoted in Hugo Martinez, *Graffiti NYC.* New York: Prestel, 2006, p. 101.

newer styles of artistic expression. Kenneth M. Lansing, a noted American art educator, fought for years for a new conception of art. He writes, "Visual art is the skillful presentation of concepts and/or emotions (ideas and feelings) in a form that is structurally (compositionally) satisfying and coherent."[100]

Lansing's wide-ranging interpretation is generally shared in the art world today and no longer excludes graffiti. But the acceptance of graffiti artists themselves began even earlier.

Graffiti Artists Are Accepted

Even as New York City officials in the 1980s were denying artists the canvases they wanted for their artwork by tightening security on subway cars, the artists themselves were becoming celebrities because of movies and other media that featured them. Artists like Sandra Fabara (Lady Pink), Jean-Michel Basquiat, Keith Haring, Lee Quiñones, Donald J. White (Dondi), Jeff Green (Doze), Fab 5 Freddy, and Leonard Hilton McGurr (Futura 2000) used their new fame to sell paintings on canvas and other artwork. But according to Fabara, one of the most famous graffiti artists of that era, many artists found it difficult to handle their new status. She says,

> At night, we're lurking round in the shadows, trying to evade the police, and the next day, you have a bunch of rich people patting you on the back and giving you wads of money, and telling you, "Great work, wonderful." It was a bit surreal, dressing like a little bum, all dirty and disgusting, and the next day in high heels and a silk dress to a party.[101]

Some graffiti artists refused to do art that could be sold in galleries because they believed it would debase graffiti's original illicit nature. However, most were happy to have the chance to make money with their art instead of having to evade police and security guards to do it. "I never really thought about my work going legal," Green admits. "Never in my wildest dreams did I think that painting subway trains would lead up to galleries and museum shows."[102] Although some of their commercial work reflects their graffiti roots, many artists went in new directions. Fabara paints lush flowers, women's faces, and bar scenes on canvas; even though they are done with spray paint, they are more complex and advanced than graffiti.

Haring was an artist who easily and quickly moved into more traditional art, partly because of his art school background. While a student at New York's School of Visual Arts in the 1970s, Haring originated a new graffiti style—chalk drawings on black paper—which he hung throughout the subway system. In 1982 when his work was exhibited at New York's Fun Gallery, Haring said he believed doing gallery work would allow people to appreciate his art more than they could have when it was illegally done in the subway system. He explains, "People who were confronted with my work could [now] take a closer and more understanding look at it and respect me as an artist."[103]

The newfound appreciation for graffiti allowed some artists to make a lot of money. Graffiti became especially popular in Europe. At an art auction in Paris, France, on June 6, 2007, a piece by McGurr sold for $34,526 and one by JonOne sold for $36,436. The most famous and highest-paid graffiti artist is Banksy. His admirers include actors Brad Pitt and Angelina Jolie, who have spent hundreds of thousands of dollars to buy his creations.

In this 2008 photo a passerby mimics a figure on this re-creation of a 1982 mural by graffiti artist Keith Haring.

Banksy's work is different from the spray-painted subway art of the 1970s that ignited the modern graffiti craze. In fact, there is a debate over whether what Banksy does is graffiti or a new form of artistic expression called street art.

Graffiti or Street Art?

Modern graffiti burst from the nozzles of spray-paint cans. Today, however, art that adorns walls and other public spaces around the world includes work in other media, including preprinted posters. Although some purists claim only stylized tags are graffiti, most people use the word *graffiti* for newer types of art that have evolved since 1990. Author Nicholas Ganz believes the newer forms of art are a logical extension of graffiti. In *Graffiti World: Street Art from Five Continents*, he writes, "Letters used to dominate but today the culture has expanded: New forms are explored [and] graffiti artists have been using a wider scope of expression. [S]tickers, posters, stencils, airbrush, oil-based chalk, all varieties of paint are used. Most artists have been liberated from relying solely on the spray can."[104]

Graffiti historian Cedar Lewisohn states that it is false to make a distinction between graffiti and street art. Lewisohn defines graffiti as "any form of unofficial, unsanctioned application of a medium onto a surface" and believes that "'street art' is a sub-genre of graffiti."[105] But of all the new graffiti forms that have evolved in recent years, the one that tests Lewisohn's flexible definition the most was devised by Evan Roth and James Powderly, who founded the Graffiti Research Lab in 2006.

Roth and Powderly both have scientific backgrounds. Roth explains, "I'm not a graffiti writer. I like to say I'm a graffiti engineer."[106] Roth and Powderly use computers, laser pens, and other electronics to display graffiti at night. At the 2008 Olympic Games in Beijing, China, Powderly and four other Americans spelled out "Free Tibet" with blue LED lights near the National Stadium. They were arrested and briefly jailed for making the political statement about China's sovereignty over Tibet. The high-tech graffiti does not permanently scar build-

GRAFFITI IS ART

When graffiti began appearing in Los Angeles in 1984, Steve Grody liked it so much that he photographed it and talked to artists who created it. Grody took pictures because he knew that graffiti could disappear within a day if someone painted over it or scrubbed it out. In his book Graffiti L.A.: Street Styles and Art, Grody discusses the city's graffiti and the culture that produced it. He also explains why he believes graffiti is art. He writes,

When I first saw spraycan graffiti [appear] in Los Angeles, I was immediately struck by [its] expressive creativity. [Regardless] of the vernacular nature of graffiti, its technical and aesthetic development has evolved to an extremely high degree. As in any art form, authority or creative expression develops through committed practice and thought. These writers may not be familiar with formal art terms such as "warm/cool split" or "figure and ground," but they use these ideas intuitively. Owing to graffiti's illegality, writers learned to paint quickly. The reason that writers use spray cans for anything beyond small tags, is that the spray can, easily concealable and portable, can cover a large area quickly, yet with control. Even though in some cases, painting may now be done in a relaxed, legal manner, the stylish and forgotten spontaneous look of the finished product comes from those roots of the movement.

Steve Grody, *Graffiti L.A.: Street Styles and Art*. New York: Abrams, 2007, p. 43.

ings, bridges, and other structures it is cast upon, and Roth and Powderly say they hope their new method will make graffiti more acceptable: "One of the goals with the Graffiti Research Lab is to try to remove some of the negative connotations that graffiti has. It's an easier pitch to sell to Mom and Dad than getting arrested every night."[107]

Newer types of graffiti may be called "neo-graffiti" or "post-graffiti" to avoid the negativity associated with the word "graffiti."

Newer types of graffiti are sometimes labeled "neo-graffiti" or "post-graffiti" as well as "street art." Sherm, a female graffiti artist from Los Angeles who also does graphic and Web design, believes people have invented new terms for graffiti because of its bad reputation. She says, "I don't know where 'street art' comes from, it seems more like a general term that the masses have come up with. Because 'graffiti' is such a bad word and has all these negative connotations attached to it still. But I've always called it graffiti because that's what my friends and all those I've known who are in this have always called it."[108]

Graffiti's poor reputation is due to the fact that it is illegal. However, many artists claim that people do not know some of the positive things that come from doing graffiti.

In Defense of Graffiti

Because written graffiti is a respected part of gang culture, graffiti has helped many young men avoid joining a gang or being harassed by gang members. As a rule, gangs respect graffiti artists, even those who are not in gangs, and leave them alone. Zuco, of Los Angeles, admits, "I got into graffiti as another way of not getting into gangs. [With] gangs, I saw people going nowhere, and why would I want to go nowhere?"[109] In the 1980s, graffiti also helped Jeff Green (Doze) stay out of trouble while growing up in New York. Green, who became a professional artist, says, "Graffiti got me on a more positive direction towards expressing myself instead of smashing a window or smashing a head."[110]

When artists talk about their craft, they always mention how hard they had to work to master graffiti. Deka, a Baltimore, Maryland, artist, said graffiti taught him the importance of having a good work ethic. Before painting graffiti, he would spend hours making and revising drawings of the pieces he created. "I would stay up crazy hours sketching," he says. "I would get a hundred page sketchbook and in a small amount of time I'd have eighty done."[111] Los Angeles artist Eklips also believes graffiti taught him positive lessons about setting goals

Graffiti artist Jeff Green (Doze) painting in his studio. He credits graffiti for giving him an artistic outlet and keeping him out of trouble while growing up.

and working hard to meet them. He says, "The best day of my life was the day my mom looked at me and she said 'I thank God for graffiti and what it's made you.' She saw that I had gained manhood and leadership through it. Graffiti [saved] my life."[112]

Haring says, "The public has a right to art. The public needs art, and it is the responsibility of a 'self-proclaimed' artist to realize the public needs art, and not to make art for the few and ignore the masses."[113] He believes that people who have never experienced art in galleries or museums benefit from seeing street art like graffiti. Journalist Kelley Moore notes how deeply graffiti has become interwoven into daily culture. She writes, "Graffiti has come a long way. Its hip, urban style has infiltrated our city streets and in many places has added a dose of art and design to even the darkest alleyways."[114] Graffiti is also ingrained in daily life from hip-hop styles to video games, like *Getting Up: Contents Under Pressure*, whose hero is a graffiti artist named Trane.

Xavier Prou, one of the world's most famous graffiti artists, is even more adamant about the power of graffiti today. He calls it "the biggest art movement in the history of the world."[115] Many people would disagree with that claim, but none can deny that graffiti is a potent form of creative expression that is here to stay.

Notes

Introduction: What Is Graffiti?

1. Merriam-Webster OnLine Dictionary, "Graffiti," 2010. www.merriam-webster.com/dictionary/graffiti.
2. Scape Martinez, *Graff: The Art & Technique of Graffiti*. Cincinnati, OH: Impact, 2009, p. 122.
3. Norman Mailer, *The Faith of Graffiti*, photographs by Mervyn Kurlansky and John Naar. New York: Praeger, 1974, p. 68.
4. Stephen Powers, *The Art of Getting Over: Graffiti at the Millennium*. New York: St. Martin's, 1999, p. 1.
5. Quoted in Monroe C. Beardsley, "The Faith of Graffiti," *Journal of Aesthetics & Art Criticism*, March 1975, p. 373.
6. Martha Cooper and Henry Chalfant, *Subway Art*, 25th Anniversary ed. San Francisco: Chronicle, 2009, p. 126.

Chapter 1: History of Graffiti

7. Robert Reisner and Lorraine Wechsler, *Encyclopedia of Graffiti*. New York: MacMillan, 1974, p. vi.
8. Robert George Reisner, *Graffiti: Two Thousand Years of Wall Writing*. Chicago: Regnery, 1971, p. 1.
9. Jean Clottes, "Rhinos and Lions and Bears (Oh, My!)," *Natural History*, May 1995, p. 30.
10. Reisner, *Graffiti*, p. 24.
11. Rodney S. Young, "Doodling at Gordion," *Archaeology*, October 1969, p. 271.
12. Quoted in Reisner, *Graffiti*, p. 64.
13. V. Pritchard, *English Medieval Graffiti*. Cambridge: Cambridge University Press, 1967, p. xiii.
14. Helen H. Tanzer, *The Common People of Pompeii: A Study of the Graffiti*. Baltimore, MD: Johns Hopkins University Press 1939, p. xii.
15. Jack Stewart, *Graffiti Kings: New York City Mass Transit Art of the 1970s*. New York: Melcher Media/Abrams, 2009, p. 13.
16. Susan A. Phillips, *Wallbangin': Graffiti and Gangs in L.A.* Chicago: University of Chicago Press, 1999, p. 21.
17. Quoted in Kristen Kammerer and Bridget Snyder, *Wisdom from the Walls*. New York: Boulevard, 1995, p. 11.

18. Reisner, *Graffiti*, p. 203.
19. Quoted in Daniel Wright, *Dear Elvis: Graffiti from Graceland*. Memphis, TN: Mustang, 1996, p. 15.
20. Wyoming State Historic Preservation Office, "The Bridger Trail: Signature Rock," Wyoming State Historic Preservation Office. http://wyoshpo.state.wy.us/btrail/signature rock.html.
21. Quoted in David Fickling, "Cave Paintings Are Graffiti by Prehistoric Yobs," *Independent* (London), February 26, 2006. www.independent.co.uk/news/science/cave-paintings-are-graffiti-by-prehistoric-yobs-467773.html.

Chapter 2: The Birth of Modern Graffiti

22. Stewart, *Graffiti Kings*, p. 13.
23. Quoted in Alexandra Chalat, "What's in a Name?" *South Philly Review*, October 4, 2007. www.southwestphilly.net/view_article.php?id=6151.
24. Quoted in Stewart, *Graffiti Kings*, p. 14.
25. Quoted in Chalat, "What's in a Name?"
26. Quoted in *New York Times*, "TAKI 183 Spawns Pen Pals," *New York Times*, July 21, 1971.
27. Quoted in Stewart, *Graffiti Kings*, p. 42.
28. Nicholas Ganz, *Graffiti World: Street Art from Five Continents*. New York: Abrams, 2009, p. 8.
29. Quoted in Dimitri Ehrlich and Gregor Ehrlich, "Graffiti in Its Own Words: Old-Timers Remember the Golden Age of the Art Movement That Actually Moved," *New York*, June 25, 2006. http://nymag.com/guides/summer/17406/#.
30. Herbert Kohl, *Golden Boy as Anthony Cool: A Photo Essay on Naming and Graffiti*. New York: Dial, 1972, pp. 9–10.
31. Quoted in Ehrlich and Ehrlich, "Graffiti in Its Own Words."
32. Jon Naar, *The Birth of Graffiti*. New York: Prestel, 2007, p. 16.
33. David Ley and Roman Cybriwsky, "Urban Graffiti as Territorial Markers," *Annals of the Association of American Geographers*, December 1974, p. 494.
34. Quoted in Cedar Lewisohn, *Street Art: The Graffiti Revolution*. New York: Abrams, 2008, p. 34.
35. Quoted in Naar, *The Birth of Graffiti*, p. 14.
36. Quoted in Mailer, *The Faith of Graffiti*, p. 78.
37. Quoted in Ehrlich and Ehrlich, "Graffiti in Its Own Words."
38. Quoted in Naar, *The Birth of Graffiti*, p. 11.

Chapter 3: Graffiti's Golden Age

39. Quoted in Lewisohn, *Street Art*, p. 42.
40. Quoted in Edward Lucie-Smith,

American Art Now. New York: Morrow, 1985, p. 48.

41. Lee Quiñones as told to Cristina Verán, "Catching Wreck," *Vibe*, August 2001, p. 39.

42. Quoted in Hugo Martinez, *Graffiti NYC*. New York: Prestel, 2006, p. 54.

43. Quoted in Mailer, *The Faith of Graffiti*, p. 69.

44. Quoted in Stewart, *Graffiti Kings*, p. 53.

45. Quoted in Naar, *The Birth of Graffiti*, p. 12.

46. Quoted in Lucy R. Lippard, *Mixed Blessings: New Art in a Multicultural America*. New York: Pantheon, 1990, p. 12.

47. Quoted in Rebecca Migdal, "Wild Style: Museum's 'Graffiti' Pays Tribute to Street 'Writers,'" *Brooklyn Paper*, June 24, 2006. www .brooklynpaper.com/stories/29/ 25/29_25graffiti.html.

48. Quoted in Canned Goods, "Ket: Graffiti Artist Interview," Canned Goods, August 2009.

49. Quoted in Ehrlich and Ehrlich, "Graffiti in Its Own Words."

50. Quoted in Stewart, *Graffiti Kings*, p. 30.

51. Quoted in Lippard, *Mixed Blessings*, p. 165.

52. Quoted in Ehrlich and Ehrlich, "Graffiti in Its Own Words."

53. Cooper and Chalfant, *Subway Art*, p. 7.

54. Quoted in Joe Austin, *Taking the Train: How Graffiti Art Became an Urban Crisis in New York City*. New York: Columbia University Press, 2001, p. 87.

55. Quoted in Lewisohn, *Street Art*, p. 30.

56. Quoted in Mailer, *The Faith of Graffiti*, p. 68.

Chapter 4: Social and Political Graffiti

57. Quoted in Colby Buzzell, "I Am Banksy," *Esquire*, December 2005, p. 198.

58. Reisner and Wechsler, *Encyclopedia of Graffiti*, 1974, p. vi.

59. Lewisohn, *Street Art*, p. 27.

60. Hermann Waldenburg, *The Berlin Wall*. New York: Abbeville Press, 1990, p. 13.

61. Tristan Manco, Lost Art, and Caleb Neelon, *graffiti brasil*. New York: Thames & Hudson, 2005, p. 10.

62. Adolf Hitler, *Mein Kampf*. Boston: Houghton Mifflin, 1999, p. 137.

63. Quoted in Martin Gilbert, *The Holocaust: A History of the Jews of Europe During the Second World War*. New York: Holt, 1985, p. 63.

64. Quoted in Diana Lambert, "Kenesset Israel Synagogue in Sacramento Struck by Vandals," *Sacramento (CA) Bee*, January 25, 2010.

65. Quoted in Aaron Gouveia, "Police Identify Upper Cape Graffiti Suspects," *Cape Cod (MA) Times*, February 10, 2010.

66. Ley and Cybriwsky, "Urban Graffiti as Territorial Markers," p. 491.

67. Quoted in Patrik Jonsson, "After Obama's Win, White Backlash Festers in US," *Christian Science Monitor*, November 17, 2008. www.csmonitor.com/USA/Politics/2008/1117/p03s01-uspo.html.

68. Xavier A. Tàpies, *Street Art and the War on Terror: How the World's Best Graffiti Artist Said No to the Iraq War*. London: Rebellion, 2007, p. 7.

69. Quoted in Jacqueline Maley, "24-7 Guard for Opera House," *Sydney Morning Herald* (Australia), March 19, 2003. www.smh.com.au/articles/2003/03/18/1047749748004.html.

70. Quoted in Trymaine Lee, "Victims Gain a Little Immortality Through Art," *New York Times*, April 19, 2007. www.nytimes.com/2007/04/19/nyregion/19mural.html?_r=1&ref=nyregion.

Chapter 5: How Modern Graffiti Spread

71. Quoted in Nograf Network, "Graffiti Art: China's Urban Nomads Target Graffiti Canvas, the Wall," Nograf Network, December 23, 2003. http://nograffiti.com/grafnews/01_07_04/graffiti_art_china.htm.

72. Quoted in Cooper and Chalfant, *Subway Art*, p. 126.

73. Cooper and Chalfant, *Subway Art*, p. 124.

74. Quoted in Lewisohn, *Street Art*, p. 44.

75. Quoted in Canned Goods, "Lyken Love: Graffiti Artist Interview," Canned Goods, September 2009.

76. Quoted in Ehrlich and Ehrlich, "Graffiti in Its Own Words."

77. Quoted in Richard S. Christen, "Hip Hop Learning: Graffiti as an Educator of Urban Teenagers," *Educational Foundations*, Fall 2003, p. 57.

78. Quoted in Steve Grody, *Graffiti L.A.: Street Styles and Art*. New York: Abrams, 2007, p. 222.

79. Quoted in SubwayOutlaws.com, "FUTURA 2000." www.subwayoutlaws.com/Interviews/Futura2000/futura_2000.htm.

80. Quoted in Art Crimes, "Os Gêmeos (The Twins)," 1999. www.graffiti.org/osgemeos.

81. Quoted in Manco, Lost Art, and Neelon, *graffiti brasil*, p. 64.

82. Quoted in Art Crimes, "Os Gêmeos (The Twins)."

83. Ganz, *Graffiti World*, p. 19.

84. Quoted in Art Crimes, "Os Gêmeos (The Twins)."

85. Quoted in Panthea Lee, "Of Spray Cans and Street Cred," Panthealee.com, April 16, 2008.

86. Quoted in Marianne Barriaux, "Graffiti Gains Ground in China," *Sydney Morning Herald* (Australia), August 21, 2009. http://news.smh.com.au/breaking-news-world/graffiti-gains-ground-in-china-20090821-etdv.html.

87. Lewisohn, *Street Art*, p. 9.

88. Quoted in Claudia Joseph, "Graffiti Artist Banksy Unmasked . . . as a Former Public Schoolboy from Middle-Class Suburbia," July 12, 2008. www.dailymail.co.uk/femail/article-1034538/Graffiti-artist-Banksy-unmasked.html.

89. Quoted in Waldemar Januszczak, "Blek le Rat, the Man Who Gave Birth to Banksy," *Sunday Times* (London), June 8, 2008. http://entertainment.timesonline.co.uk/tol/arts_and_entertainment/visual_arts/article4066727.ece.

90. Quoted in Hrag Vartanian, "Rebel Without a Crew: Street Artist Alone in Tehran," ArtCat, July 21, 2008. http://zine.artcat.com/2008/07/interview.php.

Chapter 6: Graffiti—Art or Vandalism?

91. Quoted in PBS, "Art in the Twenty-first Century: Graffiti," PBS, 2001. www.pbs.org/art21/artists/mcgee/clip1.html.

92. Quoted in Glen Helfand, "The Mission School: San Francisco's Street Artists Deliver Their Neighborhood to the Art World," *San Francisco Bay Guardian*, May 24, 2002. www.sfbg.com/36/28/art_mission_school.html.

93. Quoted in Austin, *Taking the Train*, p. 80.

94. Quoted in Bo Poertner, "City Trail Plagued by Vandals," *Lompoc Record*, February 20, 2010. www.lompocrecord.com/news/local/crime-and-courts/article_cfd4a818-1dec-11df-9308-001cc4c002e0.html.

95. Quoted in *Fiji Times*, "Vandals, Graffiti a Worry for Town." *Fiji Times*, February 18, 2009.

96. Quoted in Nograf Network, "Graffiti Art."

97. Quoted in Joel Siegel, "When TAKI Ruled Magik Kingdom," *New York Daily News*, April 9, 1989. www.zephyrgraffiti.com/otherwrt/taki183.html.

98. *Milwaukee Journal Sentinel*, "Graffiti Isn't Art: It's Just Vandalism, and Another Cost for Overburdened Taxpayers as Some Recent 'Work' Demonstrates," August 11, 2009.

99. Lawrence Alloway, "ART," *The Nation*, September 27, 1975, p. 285.

100. Kenneth M. Lansing, "Why We Need a Definition of Art," Aristos, December 2004. www.aristos.org/aris-04/lansing1.htm.

101. Quoted in Lewisohn, *Street Art*, p. 39.

102. Quoted in CNN, "From Graffiti to Galleries," CNN.com, November 4, 2005. www.cnn.com/2005/US/03/21/otr.green/index.html.

103. Quoted in Lippard, *Mixed Blessings*, p. 165.

104. Ganz, *Graffiti World*, p. 7.

105. Lewisohn, *Street Art*, p. 15.

106. Quoted in Andrew Jacobs and Colin Moynihans, "Americans Are

Arrested for Protest in Beijing," *New York Times*, August 20, 2008.

107. Quoted in Greta Dayal, "ART: Graffiti by the (Extensively Analyzed) Numbers," *New York Times*, June 25, 2006.

108. Quoted in FatCap, "Interview Sherm," FatCat.com, December 16, 2009. www.fatcap.com/article/35.html.

109. Quoted in Grody, *Graffiti L.A.*, p. 210.

110. Quoted in CNN, "From Graffiti to Galleries."

111. Quoted in Christen, "Hip Hop Learning," p. 56.

112. Quoted in Grody, *Graffiti L.A.*, p. 216.

113. Quoted in Lewisohn, *Street Art*, p. 1.

114. Kelley Moore, "Graffiti Inside the House," MSN Lifestyle, December 28, 2009. http://lifestyle.msn.com/your-home/welcome-home-blog-post.aspx?post=4123 f391-0527-4225-9da7-15e3cf19 cef7.

115. Quoted in Cooper and Chalfant, *Subway Art*, p. 124.

For More Information

Books

Craig Castleman, *Getting Up: Subway Graffiti in New York*. Cambridge, MA: MIT Press, 1982. This book details the birth of modern graffiti in New York and features interviews with many graffiti artists.

Henry Chalfant and James Prigoff, *Spraycan Art*. London: Thames & Hudson, 1987. In this book Chalfant, one of the earliest authors to write about New York graffiti, and Prigoff take a look at how graffiti has developed since the 1960s.

Nicholas Ganz, *Graffiti World: Street Art from Five Continents*. New York: Abrams, 2009. This book provides a comprehensive pictorial review of graffiti from around the world.

Tristan Manco, *Stencil Graffiti*. London: Thames & Hudson, 2002. In this book graffiti expert Manco describes graffiti done with stencils, which is popular in Europe.

Sybille Prou and King Adz, *Blek le Rat: Getting Through the Walls*. London: Thames & Hudson, 2008. In this book authors Prou and Adz profile Prou's husband, Xavier Prou (Blek le Rat), a world-famous French graffiti artist.

Internet Sources

Alexandra Chalat, "What's in a Name?" *South Philly Review*, October 4, 2007. www.southwestphilly.net/view_article .php?id=6151.

Dimitri Ehrlich and Gregor Ehrlich, "Graffiti in Its Own Words: Old-Timers Remember the Golden Age of the Art Movement That Actually Moved," *New York*, June 25, 2006. http://nymag.com/guides/summer/ 17406/#.

Roth Meas, "Graffiti Artists Teach Children the Value of Self-Expression," *Phnom Penh Post*, April 27, 2010. http://www.phnompenhpost.com/ index.php/2010042738171/Life style/graffiti-artists-teach-children- the-value-of-self-expression.html.

Films

Bomb the System, DVD directed by Adam Bhala Lough (2002; New York: Palm Pictures, 2005). American release: New York: Palm Pictures 2005.

Style Wars, DVD, directed by Tony Silver (1983; Metuchen, NJ: Plexifilm, 2005).

Wild Style, DVD, directed by Charlie Ahearn (1982; Burbank, CA: Rhino Home Video, 2007).

Web Sites

Graffiti Creator (http://graffiticreator .net). The site includes articles, interviews, images, links, and a chat forum. Visitors can write their own graffiti by using the site's computer.

Graffiti L.A. (http://graffitila.com). This site by author Steve Grody supports *Graffiti L.A.: Street Styles and Art*, his book on Los Angeles graffiti. It includes photographs, written material on graffiti, and links to other sites.

SubwayOutlaws.com (www.subway outlaws.com). This site has interviews with graffiti writers past and present, a history of graffiti, articles, pictures, and links to other sites.

Index

A

Aerosol Arabic. *See* Ali, Mohammed

Ali, Mohammed (graffiti artist), 68, 68–70

Antiwar graffiti, 66–67, *67*, 69–70

antropfagia, 81

A1one, 82, 84

Artists. *See* Graffiti writers

B

Banksy (graffiti artist), 27, 56–57, *57*, 81–82, 93

Berlin Wall, 58–59, *59*

Blek le Rat. *See* Prou, Xavier

Brazil

graffiti in, 74, 78–80

grapixo form of graffiti in, 81

political graffiti in, 59–60

Bridger, Jim, 24

Bush, George W., 69

C

Cave wall drawings/paintings, *10*, 10, 11, 13–16, *15*, 27

Cay 161 (graffiti artist), 39–40

Chalfant, Henry, 12, 38, 52, 53, 54, 72

Chauvet-Pont-d'Arc cave (France), 5, 14–15

China, graffiti in, 71, 81, 94

Christen, Richard S., 78

Cliff 159 (graffiti artist), 46

Clottes, Jean, 14–15

Cook, Brett (graffiti artist), 60

Cool Earl (graffiti artist), 30

Cooper, Martha, 52, 53, 72

Cybriwsky, Roman, 36, 65–66

D

Dali (graffiti artist), 71, 81

Deka (graffiti artist), 78, 97

Dizney. *See* Cook, Brett

Dove (graffiti artist), 77

Doze. *See* Green, Jeff

Dundes, Alan, 22

E

Eklips (graffiti artist), 97–98

El Morro National Monument (NM), 24

F

Fabara, Sandra (artist Lady Pink), 46–47, 75, 76, 72, *77*, 92

The Faith of Graffiti (Mailer), 11, 38, 46

Fear (graffiti artist), 76

Futura 2000. *See* McGurr, Leonard Hilton

G
Gang graffiti, 19–21, *21*
Ganz, Nicholas, 32–33, 80, 94
Geoglyphs, Nazca, Peru, 16–17, *17*
Getting Up (video game), 99
Gill, Anton, 63
Gillespie, Norman, 67, 69
Goldie. *See* Price, Clifford Joseph
Graceland (Elvis Presley home,
  Nashville, TN), graffiti at, 22, 23, *23*
Graffiti
  as art, 12, 33, 42, 90–91, 95
  crackdown on, 52–55, 87–88
  definition/meanings of, 8–9
  evolution of, 10–11, 42, 81
  global spread of, 12, 72–84
  golden age of, 42–51, 52, 53
  hip-hop, influence on, 72–73
  legal use of, 88, 95
  movies/other media, featured in,
    72–73, 92, 99
  Nazis, use by, 61–62
  prehistoric, 10, 13–17
  as vandalism, 8–9, 12, 52, 87, 90
  vocabulary of, 50
  written, 17–19
  See also specific types
Graffiti crews, 20, 71, 78
Graffiti World (Ganz), 32–33, 80, 94
Graffiti writers, 36
  acceptance of, 87, 92–94
  camaraderie among, 75–78
  dangers faced by, 44–47
  locations of, 38
  motivations of, 11
  rejection of term "graffiti" by, 40
Grapixo (graffiti form), 81

Green, Jeff (graffiti artist), 92, 97,
  98
Grody, Steve, 95

H
Haring, Keith, 59, 92–93, *93*, 98
Hate graffiti, 64–66, *65*, 90
Haze, Eric, 39
Hitler, Adolf, 61–62
Hobo graffiti, 26
Howard, John, 78–79

I
Independence Rock (WY), 24, *25*
Internet, growth of graffiti and,
  74
Iran, 82, 84

J
Japan 1 (graffiti artist), 39, 46
Julio 204 (graffiti artist), 31, 32
Junior 161 (graffiti artist), 31

K
Kap (graffiti artist), 39
Kidd, Bobby (graffiti artist), 30
Kilroy, James J., 26
"Kilroy Was Here," 26–27, 82
Kohl, Herbert, 34
Ku Klux Klan (KKK), 64
Kurlansky, Mervyn, 38

L
Lady Pink. *See* Fabara, Sandra
Latrinalia (bathroom graffiti), 22
Lewisohn, Cedar, 33, 58, 81, 94
Ley, David, 36, 65–66

Lindsay, John, 52
Lost Art (graffiti artist), 59–60
Lyken Love (graffiti artist), 73–74

M
Mailer, Norman, 11, 38, 46
Manco, Tristan, 59–60
Maridueña, Alain (artist Ket One),
  47, 75
Markers, as medium for graffiti, 28,
  36
Martinez, Hugo, 90, 91
Martinez, Scape, 9–10
Maze 139 (graffiti artist), 72
McCray, Darryl (artist Cornbread),
  29–30
McGee, Barry (artist Twist), 79, 80,
  85–86, *86*
McGurr, Leonard Hilton (Futura
  2000), 42, *43*, 77, 92
Mein Kampf (Hitler), 61
Michelle (graffiti artist), 39
Mico (graffiti artist), 34, 36, 40, 46,
  76
Mode 2 (graffiti artist), 73
Mompeller, Edward (artist Playboy
  Eddie), 87

N
Naar, Jon, 36, 38
Nazca geoglyphs (Peru), 16–17, *17*
Neelon, Caleb, 59–60
Neo-graffiti, *96*, 97
NOPE (graffiti artist), *29*

O
Obama, Barack, 66

Ogburn, Steve (Blade), 47, 48, 51
Oldenburg, Claes, 43
Oñate, Juan de, 24
Os Gêmeos (graffiti artists), 79–80

P
Pandolfo, Gustavo (Os Gêmeos),
  79–80
Pandolfo, Otavio (Os Gêmeos), 79–80
Petroglyphs, 16
Phase 2 (graffiti artist), 38
Philadelphia, as birthplace of modern
  graffiti, 28–30
Pichação (Brazilian political graffiti),
  74, 78–79, *79*, 81
Pictographs, 16–17
Political graffiti, 56–64
  pichação (Brazil), 74, 78–79, 81
Pompeii, *18*, 18–19
Post-graffiti, *96*, 97
Powderly, James, 94–95
Presley, Elvis, 22, 23
Price, Clifford Joseph (artist Goldie),
  72, 73, *74*
Prou, Xavier (artist Blek le Rat), 82,
  83, 99

Q
Quiñones, Lee, 44, *45*, 51, 72, 92

R
Reisner, Robert George, 13–14, 22,
  26, 58
Rodriguez, Johnny, 34
Roman Empire, 18–19
  political graffiti in, 58
Rossi, Giovanni Battista de, 18

Roth, Evan, 94–95

S
Safaitic (Arabic writing form), 17
Schjeldahl, Peter, 90
Seker (graffiti artist), 81
Seymour, Edward, 90
Sherm (graffiti artist), 97
Sic (graffiti artist), 71, 88
Signature Rock (WY), 24
Social graffiti, 6–7, 57, 60, 66
Spray paint, 28, 29, *37*
  becomes medium for graffiti artists,
    36, 42
  challenges of using, 48–49
  use of, to create 3-D effects, 49
St. Mary's Church (Walden, U.K.),
  19
Stag 161 (graffiti artist), 46
Stencils, 69, 81–83
Stewart, Jack, 19–20, 28, 49
Stewart, Michael (graffiti artist),
  46
Subway Art (Cooper and Chalfant),
  12, 52, 53, 72
Subway graffiti, 12, 39, *40*, 42–44,
  46–48, 53
  demise of, 52–55
  style of, 36, 38–39, 47–49, 51
Super Kool 223 (graffiti artist), 48, 55

T
Tag/tagging, 9, 11, 29, 34
TAKI 183 (graffiti artist), 31–32, 88, 90

Tapia-Mendoza, Juan (C.A.T.-87),
  91
Tàpies, Xavier A., 66–67
3-D graffiti, *49*, 49
Travel graffiti, 22–27

U
Urban graffiti
  evolution of, 36–39, 42, 73
  in New York, 31–34
  in Philadelphia, 28–30
  See also Subway graffiti

V
Vandalism, graffiti viewed as, 8–9, 12,
  52, 87–90

W
White, Donald J. (artist Dondi), 51,
  53, 72, 92
White Rose (German resistance
  group), 62–64
Wild Style (film), 72
Wildstyle lettering, 36, 38
World War II, graffiti of, 24, 26–27,
  61, 61–64
Writers, graffiti artists as, 11

Y
Young, Rodney S., 16

Z
Zhang Dali (Dali), 71, 81
Zuco (graffiti artist), 97–98

Picture Credits

About the Author

Michael V. Uschan has written more than seventy books, including *Life of an American Soldier in Iraq*, for which he won the 2005 Council for Wisconsin Writers Juvenile Nonfiction Award. Uschan began his career as a writer and editor with United Press International, a wire service that provided stories to newspapers, radio, and television. Uschan considers writing history books a natural extension of the skills he developed in his many years as a journalist. He and his wife, Barbara, reside in the Milwaukee suburb of Franklin, Wisconsin. He would like to dedicate this book to his nephew, budding artist Gavin Bates.